2nd edition

Jakob Freund
Bernd Rücker

Real-Life BPMN

2nd edition

Using BPMN 2.0 to Analyze, Improve, and Automate Processes
in Your Company

Jakob Freund, Bernd Rücker
Founders of Camunda
www.camunda.com

This second edition in English is based on the successful fourth German edition. Also available in Spanish.

Editing for the first English-language edition of this book was provided by James Venis of Lakewood, Colorado, USA, with assistance from Kristen Hannum. Editing for the second edition was provided by James Venis with assistance from Jalynn Venis. www.jvenis.net

Contents

Preface

Preface of the 2nd edition

"Ah, here are Mr. Freund and Mr. Rücker. Gentlemen, it's a pleasure to finally meet you! You know, I'm a real fan of your book. I especially like your method framework —it helped us a lot."

"We're glad to hear it, though we've changed that section in the new edition."

"Really? That's a shame. I liked the pyramid."

"It's a house now."

"Okay, that's reasonable. Every house has a basement —that's where we keep the IT Department. Meanwhile, up at the top, that's where you'll find me. I have a great view and, after all, I *am* the boss here!"

"Well, that's not really what we had in mind. Instead..."

"Hogwash! Anyhow, why the change?"

"Because the pyramid sometimes led to misunderstandings. For example, some people thought that *executable* process models always were refined versions of their *operational* process models."

"But that's exactly what they are! This is how our projects work, you see: The Business Department, guided by management, of course, creates an operational process model. That's the specification we send down to the basement —I mean, to the IT Department. They make it executable. It's easy for them; they just need to refine the operational model to make it executable!"

"So tell us, how well do these projects work?"

"Well, of course there are problems here and there, misunderstandings, delays, and so on. But that's just the way it is with IT. You just have to keep the pressure on!"

"What you're describing is one of the more inept approaches. That's why we changed from the pyramid to the house."

"Well excuse me! Do you have any other better ideas?"

"We do, actually. You'll find them in section 1.4.1 on page 11 of this new edition."

"Very well, I'll take a look at that. Any other news?"

"Sure. We've corrected a few mistakes, applied some improvements, and we've updated many topics to make them more current."

"More current topics? Can you give an example?"

"Among other things, we re-evaluated the relevance of the BPEL standard."

"The what?"

"Exactly."

"Is there any news about BPMN software tools?"

"Thank you for that question! Since the last edition, we have become a BPMN tool vendor. In section 6.4.2 on page 196, we describe the camunda BPM platform and our latest project: bpmn.io."

"Excuse me, are you really advertising your software here? Is that even legal? I'm disgusted!"

"But it helps to describe it all with a specific example. Otherwise, it just remains abstract theory. Besides, camunda BPM and bpmn.io are open-source projects."

"Oh, so I don't have to pay for it? Like free beer? That's great!"

"Well, that's not entirely how open source works..."

"Pah, you and your preaching again! Instead of listening to your rambling, I'll go read your book. At least that won't contradict me the whole time!"

"Enjoy!"

Jakob Freund and Bernd Rücker
September 2014

■ Preface of the 1st edition

This is a book about Business Process Management (BPM) and Business Process Model and Notation (BPMN). Truth be told, there are several BPMN books on the market, and some of them are quite good. So why should you care about this one?

This book distills the BPMN project experience that we have accumulated while running camunda, our consulting company in Berlin, Germany. Our firm specializes in BPM. During the past five years, we have applied BPMN in practically every one of more than 250 customer engagements. These were big businesses, small companies, and public institutions.

In 2009, we published the first edition of our "BPMN Hands-On Guide." According to Amazon.de, it is still the highest-ranked book on BPMN in German. We are honored by the number of five-star-ratings that readers have awarded that book. And if you read their reviews, you see that what they like best about it are the real-life examples and the vivid language. (Most German books on this topic suffer from being abstract, and the writing is uninspired.)

We joined the Object Management Group (OMG) in 2009, and we helped to finalize BPMN 2.0. We also contributed chapters to the "BPMN 2.0 by Example" tutorial that the OMG provides to beginners. These interactions showed us that, even outside of Germany, few people have applied BPMN as often, as deeply, or as broadly as have we. We decided to translate our book into English, and we gave it a cooler-sounding title than "Hands-On Guide."

We hope you'll enjoy reading this book. Even more, we hope that you will find lots of help in it —great examples, meaningful tips and suggestions, and patterns that can lead you to solutions for your own real-life BPMN challenges.

You hear people bashing BPMN once in a while with arguments that are more or less pointless. You also hear valid critiques and useful suggestions. The good news is that we have a global community of people driving BPM generally and BPMN in particular, and we thank every one of them for contributing to a standard that, while not perfect, is definitely a big step in the right direction.

Our special thanks goes to Bruce Silver, whose own book, "BPMN Method & Style," is one of those "quite good BPMN books" on the market, and to James Venis, our editor for this English-language version. If you enjoy reading it, most of your praise should go to him.

Jakob Freund and Bernd Rücker
October 2012

1 Introduction

■ 1.1 Business Process Management

This book is about Business Process Model and Notation (BPMN 2.0). To understand why BPMN was invented, we need first to understand Business Process Management (BPM).

1.1.1 Definition

Experts use different definitions for Business Process Management. We use the definition given by the European Association of BPM (EABPM) in its reference work, "BPM Common Body of Knowledge" [Eur09]:

> Business Process Management (BPM) is a systemic approach for capturing, designing, executing, documenting, measuring, monitoring, and controlling both automated and non-automated processes to meet the objectives and business strategies of a company. BPM embraces the conscious, comprehensive, and increasingly technology-enabled definition, improvement, innovation, and maintenance of end-to-end processes. Through this systemic and conscious management of processes, companies achieve better results faster and more flexibly.
>
> Through BPM, processes can be aligned with the business strategy, and so help to improve company performance as a whole thanks to the optimization of processes within business divisions or even beyond company borders.

What "end-to-end process" really means is "from start to finish." The goal is to understand and thus to assess and improve an entire process —not just its components. We find the EABPM's definition helpful because it treats automated and non-automated processes as both equally important and equally subject to the power of BPM. This understanding is essential to applying BPM successfully because it is rarely sufficient to improve only organizational procedures or the supporting technologies; most often we must improve both the procedures and the technology cooperatively.

1.1.2 BPM in practice

As consultants who specialize in BPM, our new projects almost always involve one of the following three scenarios:

1. The client wants to improve a process using Information Technology (IT).
2. The client wants current processes documented.
3. The client wants to introduce entirely new processes.

A vast majority of the time, we encounter the first scenario: the client seeks to improve a process with IT. The motivation often is a desire to improve efficiency —for example, to use software to eliminate manual keying or re-keying of data. A client may want to implement IT-based monitoring and analysis of routine processes based on key performance indicators (KPIs).

The second scenario, documenting processes, usually comes about because the client needs the documentation to guide the work of the people involved. Another rationale is that the documentation is mandated by regulation, or it is required to obtain certification such as ISO 9000.

The third scenario happens least often. We find that when companies want to introduce entirely new processes, it is usually because they are being forced to adapt to changed market conditions, develop new channels of distribution, or introduce new products.

In public announcements, companies may speak in generalities: they have an interest in exploring BPM or they want to increase their process orientation. In practice, especially in large organizations, the argument for BPM is usually well-defined and specific, but it can take two forms:

1. There is an acute reason for using BPM. The project concerns essential processes to be created, improved, or documented.
2. The reason for BPM is "strategic." There will be no direct or immediate benefit, and the project likely was initiated by some manager trying to advance his or her career.

As you can imagine, serious people don't greet the second argument with enthusiasm. It is our own experience, however, which makes us advocate strongly for this view: BPM, process management, or whatever you want to call it, is not an end in itself.

We always recommend introducing BPM in steps. Each step should yield a practical, measurable benefit that justifies the time and effort that it took to accomplish it. Once the justification of the first step is established, take the next step. You may think that this approach produces solutions isolated from each other, but what we mean to emphasize here is the controlled nature of the approach. Each step contributes to the big picture: the company's process orientation. A hiker may use a map and a compass to guide his or her steps. When you introduce BPM, you should use a good procedure model and common sense as your guides.

1.1.3 camunda BPM life cycle

Procedure models always seem to be either too simple or too complex. The too-simple ones contain only the most painfully obvious elements. They may be useful for marketing

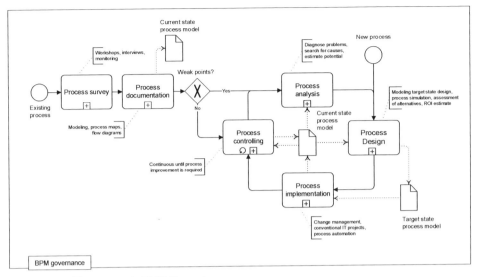

FIGURE 1.1 The camunda BPM life cycle

presentations, but not much else. On the other hand, overly complex models work so hard at anticipating every contingency that they trap the user like a fly in amber. They are unrealistically rigid. Still, without a model, we wouldn't have our "map" to orient us.

After examining the simple BPM life cycle, which is the most well-established BPM procedure model, we refined it according to our experience. We wanted to create a relatively lightweight model without too many restrictions. We thought this would be more practical than the brightly colored marketing materials we see so often at conferences and in meetings. We call ours the "camunda BPM life cycle." See it in figure 1.1.

We intend the camunda BPM life cycle to describe one process at a time. Any process can repeat independently of any other process, and the process can be at a different stage each time it repeats. The cycle triggers when one of the following situations arises:

* An existing process is to be documented or improved.
* A new process is to be introduced.

We have to start by examining an existing process. The **process discovery** clearly differentiates the subject process from other processes both upstream and downstream. The discovery reveals the output generated by the subject process as well as the importance of that output for the client. We use techniques such as workshops and one-on-one interviews to identify not only what needs to be accomplished, but also who needs to be involved, and which IT systems.

We document the findings from the process discovery in a current state process model. This **process documentation** may include many different charts and descriptions; it usually has multiple flow charts. A systematic examination of the current state process clearly identifies weak points and their causes.

We conduct **process analysis** either because first-time documentation or continuous process control has revealed a weakness of a process that cannot be remedied easily.

The causes of weak points identified by a process analysis become the starting point for another **process design**. If necessary, different process designs can be evaluated by means of the process simulation. We also conduct a process design when introducing a new process. The result in either case is a target state process model.

In reality, we normally want to **implement** the target state process model as a change in business or organizational procedures as well as an IT project. Change management, especially process communication, plays a decisive role in successful organizational change. For the IT implementation, the process can be automated or software can be developed, adapted, or procured. The result of the process implementation is a current state process corresponding to the target state process model that, conveniently, has already been documented.

In most cases, we find all the stages from process discovery to process implementation to be necessary. Because **process monitoring** takes place continuously, however, it reveals more about the ongoing operation of the process.

The most important tasks of process control are the continuous monitoring of individual process instances and the analysis of key data so that weak points can be recognized as quickly as possible. Problems with individual entities require direct remedies, and so do structural problems if that's possible. If necessary, the current state process model has to be adjusted.

If the structural causes of the problems are unclear or complex, this calls for an improvement project that —once again —starts with a systematic process analysis of the weak points. The decision to initiate such a project lies with the process owner and anyone else who depends on the process. It is common to regard continuous process control as something that follows process implementation, though it may be better to have it follow the initial documentation. This is especially true when doubt exists about the necessity of the improvement.

Given the importance of the process model within the BPM life cycle, you can imagine the importance of a modeling standard such as BPMN. Yet you may also notice that process modeling is *not* a stage in the camunda BPM life cycle. That's because process modeling is a method that affects *all* stages, especially process documentation and process design. As consultants, we constantly encounter people who try to insert process modeling as a stage at the same level as current state documentation. We think that's a misconception.

The BPM life cycle describes a simple way to achieve continuous improvement. To apply it requires coordination of the "triad." That means the responsible parties, the applied methods, and the supporting software tools. Getting the triad moving toward a common goal is the task of BPM governance, which has authority over all processes and all BPM projects in an organization.

The EABPM's definition of BPM used the term "process automation," and we've also used that term in describing the camunda BPM life cycle. BPMN was developed to automate processes better. Even if you are not an IT expert, you need to understand what process automation means because it will help you to grasp how BPMN builds bridges between business and technology.

1.1.4   Process automation

Here's a simple process: A potential bank customer mails a paper credit application, which ends up on the desk of a bank accountant. The accountant examines the application, then checks the potential customer's creditworthiness through the web site of a credit rating agency. The results are positive, so the accountant records the application in a special software —let's call it "BankSoft" —and then forwards the documents to a manager for approval.

Here's the same process automated: A potential bank customer mails a paper credit application. At the bank, a clerk scans the application into electronic form. Software called a "process engine" takes over the document and routes it to the bank accountant's virtual task list. The accountant accesses the task list, perhaps through the bank's web site or an email program like Microsoft Outlook, examines the application on screen, then clicks a button. The process engine accesses the credit rating agency, transfers the pertinent details, and receives the report. Since the report is positive, the process engine passes the information to BankSoft, and it creates an approval task in the manager's task list.

Whether this example represents optimal processing is not the point. It's here only to illustrate the following principles of process automation:

* Process automation does *not* necessarily mean that the entire process is fully automated.
* The central component of process automation is the **process engine**, which executes an executable process model.
* The process engine **controls** the process by informing humans of tasks that they need to do, and it handles the result of what the people do. (This is human workflow management.) It also communicates with internal and external IT systems. (This is service orchestration.)
* The process engine **decides** which tasks or service calls take place or not, under what conditions, and according to the result of the task execution or service call. Thus the people involved still can influence the operational sequence of an automated process.

Figure 1.2 on the next page illustrates these principles.

If you think that process automation is just a kind of software development, you are right. The process engine is the compiler or interpreter, and the executable process model is the program code. A process engine is the mechanism of choice where process automation is concerned.

* The process engine specializes in representing process logic. The services it provides would have required extensive programming in the past; using a process engine now can make you considerably more productive than before. (Or perhaps productivity is not an issue for you, and so you develop your own spreadsheet, word-processing, and drawing programs!)
* A process engine combines workflow management with application integration. This makes it a powerful tool for implementing all kinds of processes from start to end, regardless of other applications or the geography of people in the process. In some BPM software solutions, we can add a separate Enterprise Service Bus (ESB) or other components to the process engine to make the whole more versatile.

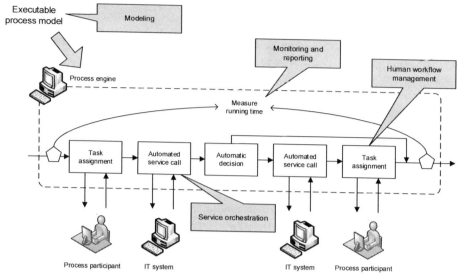

FIGURE 1.2 Process automation with a process engine

- As the process engine controls the process, it tracks everything. It always knows the current stage of the process and how long each task took to complete. Because the process engine monitors key performance indicators directly, it provides a means to analyze performance as well. This offers huge potential for successful process control.

The three features above would themselves justify implementing a process engine, but there is a fourth justification: The process engine works on the basis of an executable process model. In the best cases, this model can be developed —or at least understood —by someone who is not a technician. This promotes genuinely good communication between business and IT, and it can even result in process documentation that corresponds to reality.

This leads us to BPMN.

■ 1.2   Why BPMN?

Figure 1.3 on the facing page models a process being handled by a process engine. We created the model using an XML-based standard called Business Process Execution Language (BPEL). While some BPM products can depict BPEL graphically, BPEL defines no symbols. The resulting models fail to convey enough meaning about what's going on to help non-programmers make decisions. This has kept BPEL from being widely accepted.

When the Business Process Management Initiative (BPMI) published BPMN in 2004, the abbreviation stood for "Business Process Modeling Notation." The goal was to create process notation with standard graphics that also could be used for process automation. In 2005, the Object Management Group (OMG) took over development of BPMN. In 2011, the OMG approved version 2.0 (to which camunda contributed). Now, BPMN means

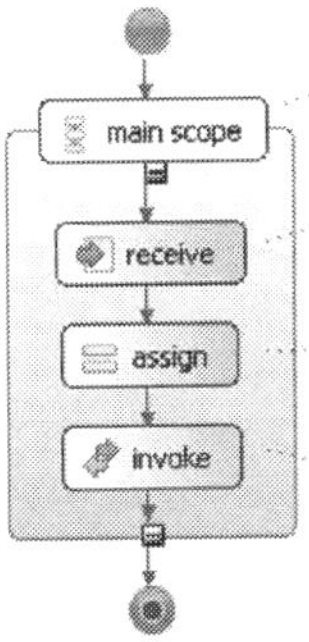

```
<?xml version="1.0" encoding="UTF-8"?>
<bpws:process name="SimpleBPEL"
  targetNamespace="http://www.camunda.com/example" ... >
  ...
  <bpws:partnerLinks>
    <bpws:partnerLink name="client"
                      myRole="SimpleBPELProvider"
                      partnerLinkType="tns:SimpleBPEL"/>
    <bpws:partnerLink name="someWebservice"
                      partnerRole="ServiceProvider"
                      partnerLinkType="tns:SimpleService"/>
  </bpws:partnerLinks>
  <bpws:variables>
    <bpws:variable messageType="tns:RequestMessage" name="input"/>
    <bpws:variable messageType="tns:InvokeMessage"  name="parameter"/>
  </bpws:variables>
  <bpws:sequence name="main scope">
    <bpws:receive name="receive"
                  createInstance="yes"
                  operation="initiate"
                  variable="input"
                  partnerLink="client"
                  portType="tns:SimpleBPEL"/>
    <bpws:assign name="assign" validate="no">
      ...
    </bpws:assign>
    <bpws:invoke name="invoke"
                 operation="methodName"
                 inputVariable="parameter"
                 partnerLink="someWebservice"
                 portType="tns:ServiceInvoke"/>
  </bpws:sequence>
</bpws:process>
```

FIGURE 1.3 Example of a simple BPEL process, graphic and as XML

"Business Process Model and Notation." Not only has the notation been defined, so has the "meta model."

The OMG is highly regarded. It is famous for the Unified Modeling Language (UML) standard used in software design. The OMG's sponsorship of BPMN adds credibility to the rationale that company managers already have for choosing a standardized model.

BPMN is a specification. It exists as a simple document that you can download for free in PDF format from the OMG [Obj11]. BPMN version 1.2 had about 320 pages; BPMN version 2.0 has about 500 pages. (Both are available only in English.) These documents define all BPM symbols, their meanings, and the rules for using them.

Before version 2.0, it was not possible to execute BPMN process models directly in process engines. Version 1.2 had not yet defined all the technical attributes required for execution, and this resulted in several unfortunate attempts to convert (or "map") BPMN models to BPEL models (see section 5.7.1 on page 175). BPMN 2.0 enabled direct execution of BPMN process models in process engines, the first important criterion in favor of its use. The second important criterion was standardization, which yields the following benefits:

- You become less dependent on certain BPM tools because you don't need to learn a new notation every time you change tools. Even now, there are more than 70 BPMN tools available (and many of those tools are free, which is wonderful, but it lowers the resistance to changing from one tool to another).

- The likelihood increases that your customers, suppliers, consultants, and so on have a grasp of BPMN and will therefore understand your process models more readily.

- When you hire new staff members, the odds are higher that they already read and can create BPMN process models.
- You can benefit from the investment made by universities and private businesses that share their advanced BPMN solutions. The BPMN framework we are going to present in the following section is an example. We never would have developed it unless BPMN was a standard.

■ 1.3   Can BPMN bridge the gap?

1.3.1   The dilemma

First, BPMN provides a set of symbols. Second, it implies a methodology that expresses itself as rules for combining the symbols graphically. Third, the symbol definitions and the rules for applying them is called syntax. Fourth, the meaning of the symbols and constructs that you can model with the symbols is called semantics.

Unfortunately, just knowing the BPMN symbols is not enough for you to create useful process models. Since 2007, we have used BPMN extensively and often, and you can believe that we have suffered terribly! Mainly, we suffered because we always tried for models with correct syntax and consistent semantics —in other words, unambiguous models. Others took the easy way out by saying, "Our process model is not really syntactically correct, and it's not really unambiguous. But that doesn't matter because the main thing is that the consumer understands it!" This attitude backfires because:

- When you apply BPMN in a syntactically incorrect way, you lose all benefits of standardization. (After all, what do you need a standard for if the models all look different in the end?) Many BPMN tools won't even enable syntactically incorrect modeling.
- Semantic inaccuracies or inconsistencies always create the risk that your model will be misinterpreted. This risk is particularly high if you create an inconsistent target state process model and then send it to IT to implement.

If you want to supply your process model directly to the process engine, you must make your model correct, precise, and consistent. At that point, you still have to reconcile two contradictory objectives:

1. Different consumers must understand and accept the process model. Making the model easy to comprehend helps to reach agreement.
2. Because the process model has to meet the requirements of formal modeling, there's usually an unavoidable level of complexity to it. This makes it harder to achieve the comprehension that leads to agreement.

Failure to reconcile the objectives, to bridge the gap in understanding between business and technology, is the main reason that process models have had limited success in the past. The really bad news is that BPMN alone also will not succeed!

Just as with spoken language, you can use BPMN and either succeed or fail. As with spoken language, successful use of BPMN depends on whom you want to communicate with and about what. You speak to your colleagues about the work you all know so well differently than you speak to your three-year-old about why the cat doesn't *like* to be pulled by its tail. Similarly, you will need other BPMN process models for coordinating with your co-workers than for presenting the future process to upper management. (Decide for yourself if the latter scenario is akin to the toddler-and-cat situation.)

On one hand, different BPMN process models are required for specific audiences and topics so that they can be understood. On the other hand, each model must contain all the detail necessary for the topic. BPMN may be a "common language" for business and IT, but the phrasing will remain different nevertheless.

The following understanding is therefore imperative for your work with BPMN:

The precision and formal correctness of the process model must vary depending on the objective of modeling and the consumers to be expected.

1.3.2   The customers of a process model

Whenever we model processes, we have to work in a customer-focused way. We must always keep the consumer of our model in mind. We must put ourselves in his or her place. This sounds simple, but few process models actually support this orientation.

As we have been saying, the knowledge, skills, and interests of the people who view our process models vary a great deal. In the following list, we have compiled the types we encounter in our BPM projects. These descriptions are for the roles played in relation to the project; they are not the titles of people in any organization. What we find is that the more experience an enterprise develops with BPM, the more consistently we see these roles fulfilled. We recommend that you become familiar with:

* **Process Owner:** Process owners have strategic responsibilities for their processes. They are vitally interested in optimizing performance. They often have budget authority, but before they sign off, they need to be convinced that your improvement plan will work. In most companies, process owners inhabit the first or second tier of management. They may be members of management committees or heads of major divisions.

* **Process Manager:** Process managers have operational responsibility for their processes. They report directly or indirectly to the process owners. They apply for improvement projects, acting as the ordering party for external services. Process managers are often low- or middle-level managers.

* **Process Participant:** Process participants work with the processes and actually create value. Their relationship to the process manager varies greatly. In companies organized by functional divisions —sales, logistics, and so on —a process manager is a functional executive for the division in which the process is carried out. Process participants report directly to that functional executive. (If the process is carried out across departments, which is common especially in process matrix organizations, see figure 1.4 on the following page, conflicts can arise between department executives. Process modeling alone cannot resolve such issues, which is why we do not examine them further in this book.)

* **Process Analyst:** The core competencies of process analysts are BPM in general and BPMN in particular. They support process managers as internal or external service

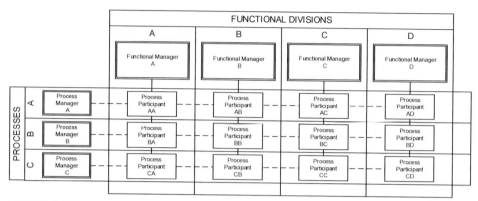

FIGURE 1.4 The process matrix organization

providers through all stages of the BPM life cycle. A process analyst may be the contact for external service providers or may act as the process manager's representative. Within the company, process analysts usually have either their own sphere of competence in BPM, such as the business organization, or they are part of their IT divisions. It is rare, however, for a process analyst to be responsible for technical implementation.

The analyst may like technical work, may know BPMN backwards and forwards, but his or her strengths are as an organizer and communicator. As the builder of bridges between business and IT, the process analyst is the center of every BPM project. About 70 percent of the people who claim or are assigned to this role, in our experience, are poorly qualified because they lack the proper analytic predisposition. The most important qualification of a process analyst is not a facility for sending out information, but a facility for receiving it. Good process analysts naturally want to understand everything thoroughly. At the same time, they have plenty of empathy in relating to the other people involved, and they can tailor their communication for every group. They remember every detail, but they also sensibly shield details from those for whom the details would just be a distraction.

Do project managers make good process analysts? No, nor should the project manager be the same person as the process analyst. Most project managers see themselves as "dynamic, action-oriented individuals" who constantly have to "get someone on board" or "pull chestnuts out of the fire." They may be extremely skilled at delegating responsibility (and honestly, some are clueless windbags). It may seem ideal to have a good process analyst also manage a BPM project, but it rarely works.

* **Process Engineer:** Process engineers use technology to implement the target state process modeled by process analysts. In the best cases, they do so in the process engine, which automates the process. You can call a programmer who programs the process logic in Java, C#, or another language a process engineer. The programmer's major work takes place during the implementation stage of the BPM life cycle, though the process analyst may get the process engineer involved at other stages as well.

Now that we've outlined the potential customers of a process model, we can talk about what the models should look like to keep these customers happy.

■ 1.4   A method framework for BPMN

In our consulting projects and workshops, we have introduced a great many people from all kinds of enterprises to BPMN. From that collected experience, we developed a practical framework for applying BPMN.

This framework helps us decide which BPMN symbols and constructs to use in which situations —and also when to hold back in the interest of simplicity. The framework focuses on projects with processes that need improved technological support and in which it is the target state that needs to be modeled. In principle, what we show as modeling patterns also can be applied to other scenarios such as the discovery, documentation, and analysis of current-state processes.

For this edition of the book, we revamped how we visualize the framework. The following section introduces the new visualization, and then we explain why we changed it. Basically, we now find fault with a widespread approach to process-focused IT projects, and we want to present an alternative that our experience suggests is better.

1.4.1   The camunda house

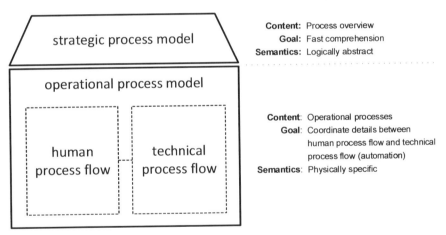

FIGURE 1.5 camunda BPMN Framework

The "camunda BPMN Framework" in figure 1.5 ("camunda house" for short) distinguishes between strategic and operational process models:

- **Strategic process model:** The primary target group for strategic process models are process owners and process managers. A secondary group early in the project may include process participants and process analysts. We provide the strategic model as a general, results-oriented representation of the process because we want to create the quickest possible understanding for an audience that has no special BPMN knowledge. We sketch the process in a few steps; we don't show errors or variations. See chapter 3 for more detailed information on creating strategic process models.

- **Operational process model:** At this level, we investigate operational details of the actual process. It may contain human or technical process flows, and we model them accordingly. A human flow is handled by a participant while a technical flow is handled by software —preferably a process engine. Of course, the human and technical flows can interact. A human may trigger a technical flow in the course of doing his or her work, as in the case of calling a software function. Equally, a technical flow may require a participant to send an email, assign a task, and so on. The human flow thus is triggered by the technical flow. We handle developing human and technical process flows in chapter 4 and chapter 5.

The camunda house is a purely methodological framework. In other words, it works independently of particular software tools, although certain tool functions may make it easier to apply. We deal with this in section 6.4.2 on page 196.

About half of this book is a detailed description of this framework. Because those chapters offer so much practical information, we encourage you to read them even if you are unconvinced of our framework's utility. If that's the case, just think of our framework as a classification system for our advice on applying BPMN practically.

Either way, we look forward to your comments and feedback, not just on this book, but also on the framework itself. By nature it's not a *perfect* approach, and it is subject to constant change and development. With your help, perhaps we can make it better for everyone!

 BPMN-Tooling

We developed the camunda house specifically to represent projects involving a lone process or a manageable group of related processes. For now, we won't deal with modeling entire process landscapes. BPMN's portfolio does not encompass process landscapes. We *have* modeled process landscapes at a customer's request (primarily, we used collapsed pools and message flows as described in section 2.9 on page 71), but we cannot recommend it. If you want a process landscape, you should use a more appropriate tool —perhaps a proprietary one that uses block arrows and rectangles and lots of colors. Of course, you can refine a process landscape with BPMN diagrams by linking the individual elements with flow charts.

1.4.2   The Great Misunderstanding

This is a confession. We declare ourselves guilty of spreading a deceptive image. The "camunda BPMN Framework" shown in figure 1.6 on the facing page was used in the previous edition of this book. Released in German in 2009 and in English in 2012, it was a huge success. Hundreds of BPMN projects used the pyramid depiction of the framework as orientation. A large international software vendor even included the pyramid in its marketing material. Unfortunately, it resulted in some misunderstandings.

In the pyramid, we distinguished between strategic, operational, and technical levels. It seems similar at first to the camunda house, but the camunda house defines the technical

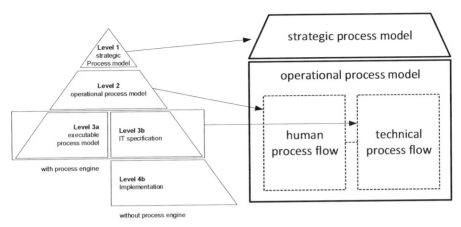

FIGURE 1.6 From old to new: The camunda BPMN Framework

level as a component called "technical process flows" within the "operational process model," and not as a level of its own. The pyramid put the "operational level" in a position equivalent to what we now call "human process flows."

This change was necessary because people too often assumed that the technical level was a refinement of the operational level, in other words, that the technical level merely added more detail. In reality, operational-level models (in the sense of the earlier framework) often are *more* detailed than their corresponding technical-level models. For example, think of a simple technical process flow —that triggers a complex manual task —which then requires a complex manual process.

Two related misunderstandings came up.

The first was a perception that the modeling on three levels had to take place in a fixed sequence, that the target-state process must be created first on the strategic level, and then on the operational level, and finally on the technical level. There's no need for that. It often makes more sense to create the operational or technical model first. Doing it this way allows you to develop a clearer understanding of the way process participants will have to do their work before you attempt to summarize or abstract it into a strategic process model. It is, in fact, common practice to conceive the technical and human flows of a process model *concurrently*, for example, in a workshop.

The second misunderstanding related to a strict separation of responsibilities. It was assumed that only the business side would define the strategic and operational levels while only the IT Department would define the technical level. We found this assumption most frequently in enterprises with difficult political situations, where cooperation between IT, operations, and business departments was less than ideal.

We should all understand that even a technical flow represents a "business model." After all, it describes business requirements. It differs from a classic request document only in that the technical flow anticipates the executable source code —a major advantage of BPMN. The risk in such a strict segregation of responsibilities is that the technical model, while compliant with requirements, may become incomprehensible and unsatisfactory to the business.

It is a similarly serious matter not to involve IT sufficiently in the design of human processes. To believe that you can define a process purely from an operational perspective and only *then* align the technical implementation with it is ... naive. Experience shows us repeatedly that operational decisions can and should be influenced by technological realities, either because what the business wants is technologically impossible (or perhaps infeasible for cost reasons) or because the technology can offer solutions that are not "on the radar" for the people defining operational requirements.

To summarize, you could say that the operational process model belongs both to the business and to IT. As a shared artifact, both parties should share in its development.

What does this thinking mean in terms of our approach to projects? Basically, it aligns with that of agile project organizations: The strict separation of concept from realization is as outmoded as the classic waterfall pattern of development. Most IT projects go better with iterative development, either in "sprints" within a "scrum" or otherwise, and it doesn't matter if the project is about process improvement or automation. The business and IT shouldn't work in isolation.

To be abundantly clear: Project participants may need to be shaken out of their comfort zones and motivated sufficiently to work honestly with "the other side." In our engagements during the last few years, the result of our strong encouragement for cooperation always has been the same: massive amazement at how productive a project can be. When IT and the business work side-by-side to define the target-state process at the strategic and operational levels, *including* technical flows, the technical flows can become executable within days or even hours.

As Thorsten Schramm of LVM Versicherung (a large insurance firm) put it during one of our workshops:

"It took only a few days to highly inspire the whole project team (consisting of people from both IT and business departments) for process mapping with BPMN 2.0, so right now the first improved processes are already emerging."

Thorsten distills our message nicely. Sometimes, the cooperation experienced within a workshop is just as meaningful as learning the BPMN 2.0 methodology. BPMN thus can operate synergistically to produce positive change within the enterprise.

2

The notation in detail

■ 2.1 Understanding BPMN

What does a monkey know about the taste of ginger?

This Indian proverb expresses the truism that you can't fully appreciate what you don't understand. We see a corollary in the English expression, "Don't cast pearls before swine."

BPMN is a pearl not everyone can appreciate because not everyone understands it. If you are new to the standard, you won't regret spending some time to familiarize yourself with its underlying principles. For those who already know the BPMN specification, this chapter provides explanation and tips beyond the specification itself. It also describes the visual conventions we use when applying symbols. This is our BPMN etiquette.

A full understanding makes BPMN an extremely powerful tool for any modern BPM project. In our experience, however, even those with high confidence in their BPMN knowledge still may fail to understand certain fundamental principles, and they often express surprise that sequence flows must not be drawn across pool boundaries.

2.1.1 Things BPMN does *not* do

BPMN was developed to model processes: logical, chronological sequences of events. That's all. Nonetheless, you often hear BPMN criticized for *not* representing:

- Process landscapes
- Organizational structures
- Data
- Strategies
- Business rules
- IT landscapes

We appreciate how important it is to incorporate these topics into process documentation. We also know that many process professionals come from the systematic world of Architecture of Integrated Information Systems (ARIS) (see section 2.12.1 on page 82). They have worked with event-driven process chains (EPCs), and they may regard BPMN as insufficient. But feasible (and even partly standardized) notations exist for the topics in the list above, and we are glad for it! It relieves BPMN of over-complication and keeps BPMN from being a monstrosity that nobody would want to compile, develop, or even understand. We remind those professionals that:

- BPMN process models are easy to combine with other types of diagrams. It is just a question of the tools used.
- BPMN provides extension options, including custom symbols. We explain this in section 2.11.2 on page 81.

Obviously it would be wonderful if BPMN could provide a complete, out-of-the-box alternative for the ARIS methodology. We admit that's not the case for the pure standard, but precisely because BPMN *is* a standard, software tools are now being created to use BPMN for the other necessary views.

2.1.2   A map: The basic elements of BPMN

When you draw a process diagram in BPMN, you use symbols that can be assigned to the categories shown in figure 2.1. We refer to these categories as the basic elements of BPMN.

In general, certain tasks have to be carried out during a process (*activities*), perhaps under certain conditions (*gateways*), and things may happen (*events*). What connects these three flow objects are *sequence flows*, but only within a *pool*. If connections cross pool boundaries, the process resorts to *message flows*.

Furthermore, *artifacts* provide additional information on the process, but these cannot influence the order of flow objects directly. Every artifact can connect to every flow object

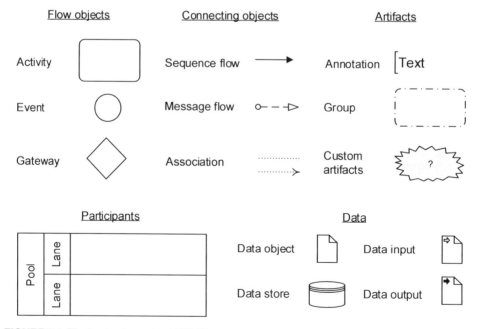

FIGURE 2.1 The basic elements of BPMN

through *associations.* (You can also incorporate your own symbols as additional artifacts into a BPMN palette all your own. We detail this option in section 2.11.2 on page 81.)

BPMN 2.0 contains an additional **data** category. This refers to the creation, processing, and filing of information that may become relevant within the scope of process handling, thus the category's symbols usually connect to activities through associations.

There are three more aspects necessary to a full understanding of BPMN:

- The advanced ideas and rules behind this simple scheme
- The full range of symbols and
- The practical know-how to apply this stuff

The ideas and rules and the full range of symbols are explained later in this chapter. The practical know-how is acquired through experience, but we offer our knowledge in the subsequent chapters to help speed your progress. We've also devised a few "recipes" for applying BPMN. They may help you to avoid some traps that often snare beginners.

2.1.3   Perspectives in process analysis

Someone accustomed to modeling processes with other notation systems may have trouble adjusting to an extremely important aspect of BPMN: everything depends on perspective.

BPMN is based on the assumption that one or more *participants* can exist within one diagram. Do not, however, jump to the conclusion that a participant functions like a role, a department, or an employee! In BPMN, a participant is a *logical* element to which the following rules apply:

- There can be only one participant for each process. (This means logical participants; there may be many human participants.)
- The participant has complete control over the process flow.
- The participant is fully responsible for its process.
- Other participants cannot influence a participant's process; they may not even know how it works.
- If a participant wants to interact with other participants within the context of the process, the participant must communicate with the others, and they affect their own processes accordingly.

The same process may look completely different for each participant, and how it looks depends on its perspective. This results in different process models.

In BPMN, the symbol for a participant and for its process is the pool; each process gets its own pool. Logically, however, a participant can control more than one process.

If you learn to handle pools properly, you will have mastered the most significant principle of process modeling —assuming you're aiming for modern BPM aligned with necessary business IT. In section 2.9 on page 71, we detail this subject and also solve the riddle of why there can be only one logical participant for each process.

2.1.4　Models, instances, tokens, and correlations

In the specification for BPMN 2.0, Chapter 7 contains a new section titled *Understanding the behavior of diagrams*. It introduces the idea that the behavior of the diagrams must be understood as well as the processes they describe. (Note: Because a diagram may contain several pools, a single diagram implies *n* processes). This is easier in theory than in practice because some process models are so complex that it becomes hard to know how to handle some circumstances. Remember the following:

- **Process model**: The basic description of a process. A diagram may describe one or more process models.

- **Process instance**: A process carried out in reality —what a layperson calls an "operation." A customer complaint is an instance of a complaint process, for example. Some processes may be instantiated only a few times in a year, such as end-of-quarter reporting in the accounting department. Other instances occur more often. Think of the millions of credit-report requests in a year's time.

- **Token**: You can apply the token model, if you have a process model in mind and want to find out which process paths must or may be used during a process instance. A token is a concept we compare to a car: A car follows a road. At an intersection, its driver must decide to continue in a straight path or to turn left or right. Or perhaps the car turns *and* a clone of the car continues straight on. This is where the car metaphor breaks down, but we hope you get the gist: that the road system corresponds to a process model and that any particular route the car takes represents an instance. The token model can help you understand even the most complex BPMN process models, so tokens are also explained in the above-mentioned section of the BPMN specification. We apply this method frequently in examples throughout this book.

- **Correlation**: Do you ever get letters with a transaction key or a file number? When you reply, you are expected to reference the key or number to make it easier for your correspondent to allocate your communication properly. This allocation based on an unambiguous key is called correlation. Another example is when you pay a bill, and you are asked to write the invoice number on your check. If you don't comply, your payment may not be properly allocated, and the lack of correlation can lead to reminder notices, late-payment fees, and other unpleasantness. Correlation is often crucial to the success of processes, from both organizational and technical points of view. Some of the costliest mistakes come from carelessness with the issue of appropriate correlation.

2.1.5　Symbols and attributes

The BPMN specification describes the symbols provided for process modeling. It also describes the many attributes that you can assign to the symbols. Many of these attributes don't appear in diagrams, though they are stored in the modeling tool and used when a process engine executes the modeled process.

2.2   Simple tasks and none events

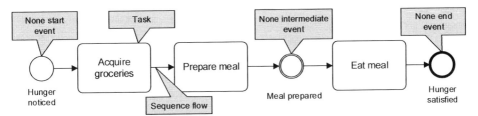

FIGURE 2.2 Our first process

Figure 2.2 shows a simple process triggered by someone being hungry. The result is that someone must shop for groceries and prepare a meal. After that, someone will eat the meal and have his or her hunger satisfied. You will easily recognize the following symbols and their meanings in the diagram:

Tasks

Tasks are the heart of the process. Ultimately, something has to happen to bring about a desired outcome. In BPMN, a task technically is part of the activities category, which also includes the subprocess explained in section 2.8 on page 59.

 Our BPMN Etiquette

When naming tasks, we try to adhere to the object-oriented design principle of using the [verb] + [object] pattern. We would say "acquire groceries," for example, not "first take care of shopping for groceries." ∎

Events

Events describe significant things that happen before, during, or at the end of a process. The example in Figure 2.2 uses only "none events." None events can be used in a process flow to indicate a status or a milestone. We explain about more event types later.

- **Start events** show which event causes the process to start.
- **Intermediate events** stand for a status that is reached in the process and that is modeled explicitly. They are used infrequently, but intermediate events can be useful, for example, if you regard reaching a certain status as a milestone and you want to measure the time until the milestone is reached.
- **End events** mark the status reached at the end of the process path.

Even for these simple events, we have to make further distinctions:

- Start events are catching events. That means something happened independent of the process, but the process has to wait for this event, or react to it.
- Intermediate events may occur, or they may be caused or triggered by the process itself (throwing events). The none intermediate event marks a status reached by the process and is therefore a throwing event. (Again, we will explain about more event types later, including more types of intermediate events to be classified as catching events.)

■ End events take place when the process can no longer react to them. As a consequence, only the process can trigger them.

 Our BPMN Etiquette

Events refer to something that has already happened regardless of the process (if they are catching events) and as a result of the process (if they are throwing events). For this reason, we use the [object] and make the [verb] passive in voice, so we write "hunger noticed." BPMN does not require you to model start and end events for a process —you can leave them out —but *if* you model a start event, you must model an end event for each path. The same is true for end events that require start events. We always create our models with start and end events for two reasons: first, that way it's possible to determine the process trigger, and second, you can describe the final status of each path end. We only sometimes abandon this practice with subprocesses. More on this later.

Sequence flows

The sequence flow describes the time-logic sequence of the flow elements: tasks, events, and the gateways we describe later.

The process path taken by our token is also a sequence flow. It is "born" with the process instance because of the start event. Through the sequence flow and by means of the tasks and the intermediate events, it reaches the end event, where it is "consumed" and disappears. This also leads to the "death" of our process instance.

 Our BPMN Etiquette

We always draw our process diagrams horizontally, from left to right, but there is nothing to keep you from orienting your flow differently. You may orient your diagrams vertically instead of horizontally, for example, although that is unusual.

■ 2.3   Design process paths with gateways

2.3.1   Data-based exclusive gateway

Certain things can only be done under certain circumstances, so few processes always take the same course.

In our simple example (figure 2.3 on the next page), we want to go into the details of cookery. Driven by hunger, we think about what we are going to cook today. We only know three recipes, so we choose one. We can either cook pasta *or* cook a steak *or* prepare a salad. Let's say that these options are exclusive —we will never prepare more than one at a time. The point of decision on what to do next is called a "gateway." We decide based on available data (the chosen recipe) and we follow only one of the paths, which is a data-based exclusive gateway. We abbreviate "exclusive gateway" as **XOR**.

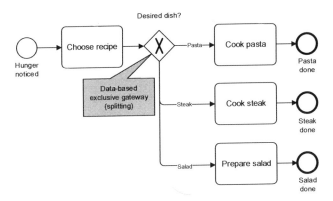

FIGURE 2.3 The XOR gateway.

Bear in mind that a gateway is not a task! You have to determine facts and needs before reaching a gateway. We will encounter this again in Business Rules Management (see section 4.5.4 on page 135).

$$\langle X \rangle = \langle \rangle$$

FIGURE 2.4 Both symbols mean the same.

BPMN uses two symbols for XOR gateways (see figure 2.4). They are identical in meaning. We always use the version with the X because it seems less ambiguous, but use what works for you.

 Our BPMN Etiquette

As in figure 2.3, we place the crucial question before the gateway. This is our convention, which has proved its value in our projects. Possible answers go on parallel paths after the gateway, which is how the BPMN specification shows them. We always work with XOR gateways as follows:

1. Model the task that requires a decision for the XOR gateway.

2. Model the XOR gateway after that. Create a question with mutually exclusive answers.

3. Model one outgoing path (or sequence flow) for each possible answer, and label the path with the answer.

An XOR gateway can have as many outgoing paths as you like. We start some paths in the upper left corner and the others in the bottom left corner, but these are just our style conventions.

By the way, it is not unusual to have three end events nor for the process to result in three end states. Recognizing this possibility can help you with more complex diagrams. Later, we will give more reasons for working with different end events. BPMN is not a block-oriented process notation, so you need not merge a split process path later —you can, but you don't have to.

Certainly, it may make semantic sense to merge the three paths. The meal is eaten after it's prepared, regardless of the recipe chosen. We can use the XOR gateway for merging also, and doing so leads the tokens from the three incoming paths into a single outgoing path. (See figure 2.5.)

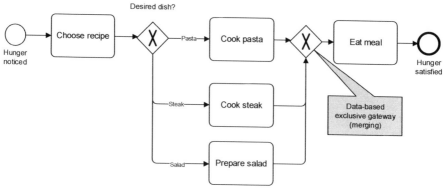

FIGURE 2.5 XOR gateways can also merge.

The double application of the XOR gateway —splitting and merging or "XOR split" and "XOR merge" —may confuse beginners. You can even model an XOR gateway that merges *and* splits at once! (See figure 2.6.) You have to decide if you prefer to compact your diagrams this way. For our part, we usually choose not to do that, and instead draw the two XOR gateways in succession. This method prevents misinterpretation.

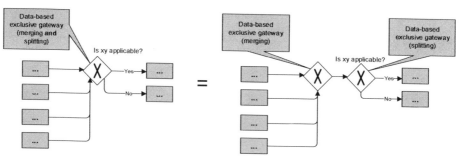

FIGURE 2.6 Two ways of representing a combined merge/split.

2.3.2   Parallel gateway

Suppose that now we want a salad on the side. If you want salad no matter what, you could model it as we have done in figure 2.7 on the next page.

Here, we've introduced another symbol, the (text) annotation. This is an artifact that you can associate with any flow object (in this case, tasks). You can enter any text; in our

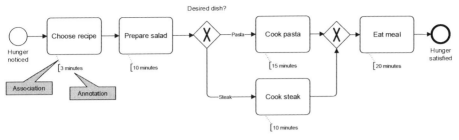

FIGURE 2.7 Preparing salad and main course.

example, we entered the average time to carry out the associated task. The total of the task times equals the running time of the process, which was a total of 48 minutes for pasta and 43 minutes for steak. Congratulations: you've just analyzed your first process based on key data!

Still, this means waiting 23 or even 28 minutes until you can start to eat. Insufferable! You're really hungry, but what can you do? Maybe you don't prepare the salad first and then cook the pasta or the steak, but you work on both at the same time —in parallel. The appropriate symbol is the parallel gateway, or the "AND gateway" for short, as shown in figure 2.8.

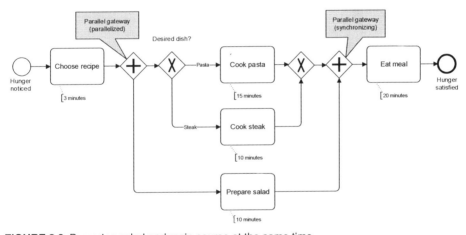

FIGURE 2.8 Preparing salad and main course at the same time.

Diagramming tasks as parallel does not make simultaneous processing compulsory. In contrast to the example shown in figure 2.7, it is also not imperative that you prepare the salad before starting other tasks. Parallel preparation does, however, reduce our total time by 10 minutes. It is classic process optimization to make tasks parallel as much as possible.

As the example shows, the process is not only parallel (it uses an "AND split"), but the paths also synchronize later (an "AND merge"). The reason is easy to understand: you can only start to eat after both main course and side dish are prepared.

How would the concept of tokens apply to an instance of this process? The token is "born" at the start event, it runs through the "choose recipe" task, and then it plunges into the AND split. One token emerges from the gateway for each path. That means two tokens in this example: The first token enters the XOR split, and its outgoing path depends on the recipe selected.

Let's assume we want to cook pasta. The token enters the task and stays there 15 minutes. At the same time, the second token enters the second, "prepare salad" task, where it stays only 10 minutes. After 10 minutes, it moves on to the AND merge. The number of incoming paths determines the number of related tokens the gateway is waiting for, so here, it waits for two tokens of the same process instance.

In our scenario, the second token arrives at the AND merge after 10 minutes, while the first token stays in "cook pasta" for a total of 15 minutes. This means the AND merge waits until the first token arrives —an additional 5 minutes. At that point, the tokens happily merge into a single token, which continues on the outgoing path.

Does that sound too abstract or technical? It is not. The AND merge behavior is identical to your own: The salad is ready, but the pasta is not, so you wait. When the pasta finally is ready, you eat.

Why the seemingly complicated token concept then? Think of 90 million process instances created by credit agencies, for instance, every year. Surely, these aren't executed in strict sequence. They overlap. To define and carry out such complex processes and their various parallel operations, branchings, mergings, and synchronizations correctly every day, the token approach is not only extremely helpful in conceptual design and implementation, but also necessary. We hope it is clear by now that process instances are not identical to tokens: Many tokens can run within the bounds of a single process instance.

Check your understanding with the following questions:

Question: Figure 2.9 shows the same process, but the AND merge was left out for lack of space, and the path from the "prepare salad" task leads directly to the XOR merge. What happens if we instantiate the process, and we decide in favor of pasta?

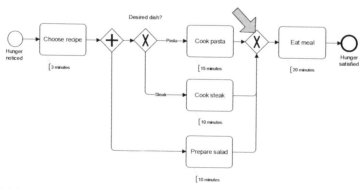

FIGURE 2.9 What happens in this process?

Answer: The token is generated and then cloned as always at the AND split. As soon as we finish preparing the salad, the token passes through the XOR merge and "eat meal" executes. Five minutes later,"cook pasta" also completes. Its token passes through the XOR merge and "eat meal" executes again! That's not the behavior we wanted.

Question: Figure 2.10 shows a process that consists of two tasks only. Once instantiated, how long does the process instance live?

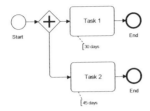

FIGURE 2.10 How long does the process instance live?

Answer: It lives 45 days, which corresponds to the run time of the process. Even though the token generated in the AND split passes through task 1 after 30 days and then is consumed by the upper end event, the second token stays in task 2 for an additional 15 days. The process instance continues to live until the second token is consumed by the lower end event.

Note: As long as just one token lives within the process, the process instance lives too! The instance cannot finish until all tokens generated are consumed.

2.3.3   Data-based inclusive gateway

We want to make our process even more flexible: When we are hungry, we want to eat

* Only a salad,
* A salad and "something real," like pasta or steak, or
* Only something real.

Using the symbols you have learned so far, you could model the situation as shown in figure 2.11.

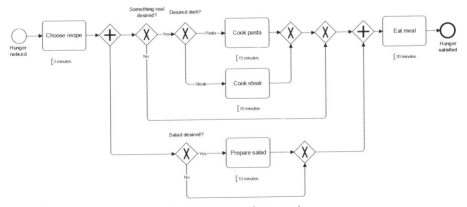

FIGURE 2.11 Various options in the combination of our meal.

If you want a more compact representation, you can use the data-based inclusive gateway —the OR gateway for short. (See figure 2.12.) Use OR gateways to describe and/or types of situations, in which processing can flow along one, many, or all outgoing paths. OR gateways can keep diagrams from becoming overly complex.

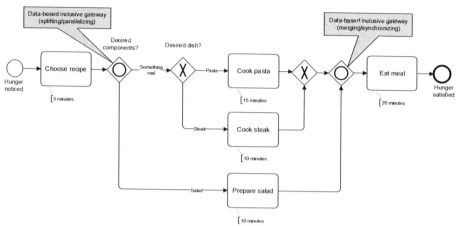

FIGURE 2.12 The OR gateway enables the compact representation of complex path variants.

We can use OR gateways to combine paths too: Depending on whether we want to eat just a salad *or* something real, or a salad *and* something real, we have to wait either for one token to arrive (merge) or for both tokens (synchronize) before we can eat. Note the difference between this and figure 2.11 on the preceding page, however. In the version without the OR gateway, we could have resolved not to prepare anything (neither salad nor something real), but we ate after this decision. The OR gateway excludes this absurdity. We have to decide at least in favor of a salad and/or something real, otherwise the token gets stuck in the gateway. Strictly speaking, the BPMN specification determines that a runtime error occurs in such a case, and that's important when it comes to technical process implementation.

In practice, handling OR gateways is not as simple as these examples imply. It's easy to understand that progress depends on waiting for another token to reach an OR merge. It can be harder to trace the synchronization rules with complex diagrams that sprawl across several pages. Just memorizing the conditions that apply at the OR split isn't a solution.

Consider figure 2.13 on the next page: whether the OR merge needs to synchronize or not depends on whether the OR split runs through one or more paths. Here's the scenario: The first token reaches the OR merge after 30 days. Because answer 2 applied to the previous OR split too, another token is on its way, and it will stay in task 2 for another 15 days. This task is completed, so it becomes possible that a decision made at the XOR split results in the second token being routed through the answer 1 path, and being consumed by the end event. What happens to the first token at the synchronizing OR merge? *The OR gateway must register that the second token has vanished, and it must forward the first token.*

This could cause problems in three circumstances:

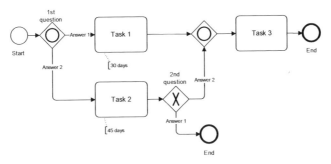

FIGURE 2.13 How long does the second gateway have to wait?

- You come across an OR merge in your process manual on page 10, and you have to rummage through the previous 9 pages to understand what conditions require which waiting times.
- You implement such a process in an organization that makes a person responsible for task 3 but permits that person no control over the process.
- A process engine runs the process and controls the synchronizing behavior. It is expensive to implement such a check, and it is bound to fail. In some cases it may be impossible.

There are a couple of reasons for using the OR gateway —with caution.

Question: Can we model the process as shown in figure 2.14?

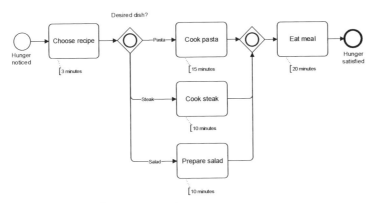

FIGURE 2.14 An incredibly (?) compact version.

Answer: Sure, this makes the model more compact, but it changes the meaning. This process model produces the following outcomes:

- We eat only pasta.
- We eat only steak.
- We eat only salad.
- We eat pasta and salad.
- We eat steak and salad.

* We eat pasta and steak.
* We eat pasta, steak, and salad.

And the last two outcomes aren't what we intend!

2.3.4   Default flow and getting stuck

There's another aspect to working with XOR and OR gateways. (To simplify matters, let's set the salad aside for now and focus on real meals.) What happens if we want neither pasta nor steak? In the previous models, this situation meant that our token could never get beyond the XOR split for "desired dish." According to the BPMN specification, that "throws an exception." In other words, a runtime error occurs.

Don't get angry because we are talking about throwing exceptions! (We'll come back to this issue and show why it doesn't concern only IT.)

The so-called default flow protects us from runtime errors. We indicate the default flow with the small slash shown in figure 2.15. The principle behind default flows is simply that all outgoing paths are examined; when none of the other paths apply, the process uses the default. Don't mistake the default flow for the usual flow, however. The symbol does not mean that the default applies most of the time. That's a different question.

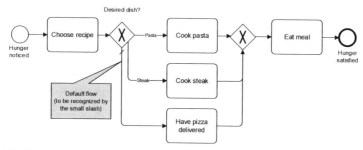

FIGURE 2.15 The default flow.

   Our BPMN Etiquette

You don't have to use a default flow, of course. You can draw a normal sequence flow instead and label it "other" or whatever you like. We use the default flow any time there's a risk of getting stuck, and we want to avoid disruption to the organization. If a diagrammed decision has Yes or No outflows only, risk is zero; more complex decisions present greater risk.

In our models, default flows help us to determine if we have limited the risk of getting stuck. In terms of aligning business and IT goals, this is certainly good business practice.

2.3.5   Complex gateway

The complex gateway is a category apart. While it isn't used often, there are situations that justify its use. An example: we want to order pizza. We peruse the menu of our favorite supplier, but just for a change, we also look on the Internet. Once we find something we want to try after researching *both* sources, we order the pizza.

How can we model that? The attempt shown in figure 2.16 results in ordering the pizza only after the research in *both* sources completes.

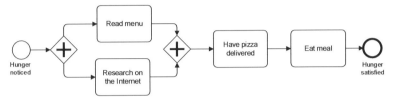

FIGURE 2.16 Pizza research with AND merge.

In figure 2.17, neither is an option: Based on the token concept, we would execute the "order pizza" task twice. (Remember the test question in section 2.3.2 on page 22?)

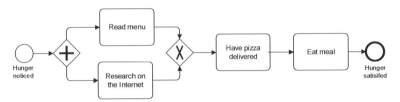

FIGURE 2.17 Pizza research with XOR merge.

Nor does the OR merge in figure 2.18 solve the problem: When a token arrives at the OR merge, the process waits for corresponding tokens that may never get there. The OR merge behavior is thus the same as an AND gateway.

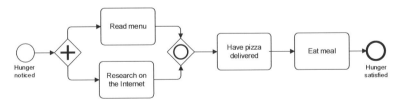

FIGURE 2.18 Pizza research with OR merge.

The solution is the complex gateway combined with an annotation, as shown in figure 2.19 on the following page. As soon as one of the two tasks completes, the complex merge sends the token to the "order pizza" task. When the next token reaches the complex merge, it is consumed. It vanishes.

Here's a similar situation: Assume we execute four tasks at once. There's a fifth task to execute once three of the first four tasks complete. For example, we ask four friends what

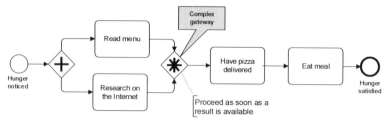

FIGURE 2.19 Pizza research with complex merge.

pizza place they want to order from. Once three friends have offered opinions, we decide. We can model our synchronizing behavior with a complex gateway. (See figure 2.20.)

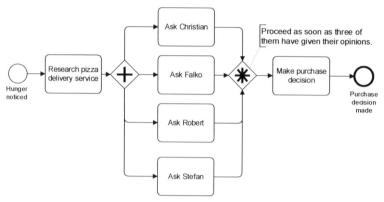

FIGURE 2.20 Using complex gateways to realize *m* out of *n* merges.

In principle, a complex gateway also can be applied as a split —to summarize several different gateways in one symbol to save some space, for instance. The OR split from the process in figure 2.14 on page 27 could be replaced with a complex gateway by writing the split semantics in an annotation. That doesn't really make sense, though, and we have never used the complex gateway as a split nor seen it used in any practical model.

■ 2.4 Design process paths without gateways

Some people don't like gateways. They think gateways make process diagrams too comprehensive or even inflated, and they would rather do without all those diamonds. While gateways *are* optional —you can instead model the logic of the XOR, AND, and OR gateways directly with the tasks —you have to be careful. It's rare that you can eliminate gateways entirely.

Figure 2.21 on the next page illustrates an alternative to the OR split as well as to the XOR merge. The upper and the lower process models are equivalent, but the upper model

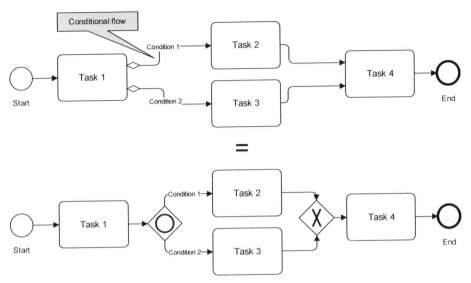

FIGURE 2.21 OR split with conditional flows and XOR merge.

shows two flows routing directly to task 4. It also represents the OR split with conditional flow symbols: the small diamonds connected to task 1. Conditional flow symbols may connect only to tasks or subprocesses, and only as outlets. They may not be used with gateways or events.

If you read section 2.3 on page 20 carefully, you likely see the problem with this: If only one of the two conditions applies, everything is okay, but if both apply, they generate two tokens in the OR split and so trigger task 4 twice thanks to the XOR merge. This isn't necessarily wrong, but it probably isn't intended. And that brings us to the first problem associated with gateway abstinence:

We cannot model synchronizations (that is, AND merges) without gateways.

The second problem is that we can't combine conditional checks. We can't represent the process logic shown in figure 2.22 without gateways because of the intermediate event.

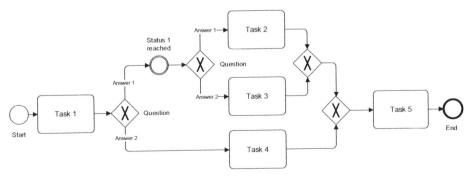

FIGURE 2.22 Combined XOR gateways.

The third problem is that conditional flows follow the same semantics as the OR split. In other words, the defined conditions must not exclude each other. Because the OR split is compatible with the subsequent XOR split, this isn't crucial, but modelers and those who use their diagrams need to be aware of this. Otherwise, in our experience, misunderstandings quickly result.

Would it be better to use gateways all the time? No, there's no need for that either. A simple loop, for example, can be better off without XOR merges because it's less confusing for the inexperienced. And because BPMN permits multiple flows from start events to end events, the diagrams can be nicely compact. We modeled the process in figure 2.23 with and without gateways to illustrate this. (Yes, technically speaking, the models are not identical: The upper one includes the XOR gateway syntactically, so several paths must be used. It requires that conditions 1 and 2 never occur at the same time. This is not the case in the lower model, where both conditions can apply.)

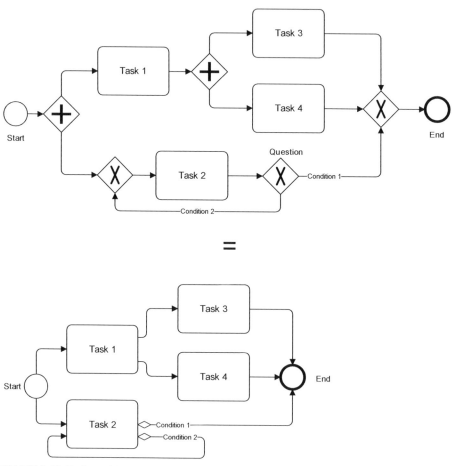

FIGURE 2.23 Both models describe (almost) the same process.

2.5   Lanes

We have talked about *what* to do in our processes, but we have not yet explained *who* is responsible for executing which tasks. In BPMN, you can answer this question with lanes.

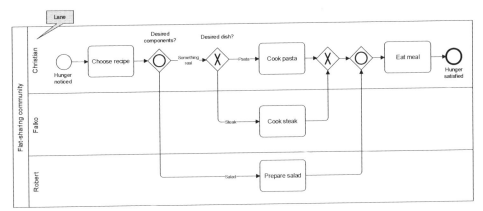

FIGURE 2.24 Responsibilities represented using lanes.

Figure 2.24 shows that the tasks in our sample process were assigned to particular people. We can derive the following process description from the assignments: If Christian is hungry, he chooses a certain recipe. Depending on what Christian chooses, he can either take care of it himself (cook pasta), or he can get his roommates on board. If the latter, Falko cooks steak and Robert prepares salad. In the end, Christian eats. The three lanes (Christian, Falko, Robert) are united in one pool designated "flat-sharing community." (We discuss pools in detail in section 2.9 on page 71.)

In the example, lanes equate to people, but this meaning is not specified by BPMN. You can designate the lanes as you like. In practice, lanes are often used to assign:

- Positions in the primary organization, for example, accounting clerk.
- Roles in the secondary organization, for example, data protection officer.
- General roles, for example, customer.
- Departments, for example, sales.
- IT applications, for example, CRM system.

BPMN-Tooling

Some tools enable you to assign the elements in your diagram to different categories or views, such as executing positions, responsible positions, supporting IT applications, and so on. You can also show the process from the respective view. This changes the lanes, and arranges the elements accordingly.   ■

Incidentally, lanes have a long history in the world of process modeling. They're analogous to a swimming pool in which swimmers swim only in the lanes to which they are assigned. Swimlane representations are common to different process notations.

In BPMN, lanes can also interlace to illustrate refined responsibilities. (See figure 2.25.)

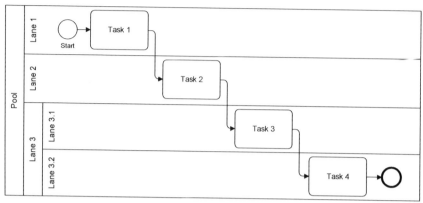

FIGURE 2.25 Interlacing lanes.

 Our BPMN Etiquette

BPMN does not specify that you have to order tasks either vertically or horizontally. In figure 2.25, the process starts in the top left corner and ends in the bottom right, and that is our convention, but you can model it from the bottom left to the top right as well. The essential thing is that you decide on a style for structuring your diagrams, and then apply it consistently. Keeping to your standard makes your diagrams easier to read from one to the next.

Handling lanes often is trickier than you may expect. In our little process, for example, we assume that the tasks are clearly distributed. But what if Falko and Robert want to eat too? A representation like that in figure 2.26 would be syntactically wrong. It is not permissible to have a flow object (activity, event, gateway) positioned outside a single lane.

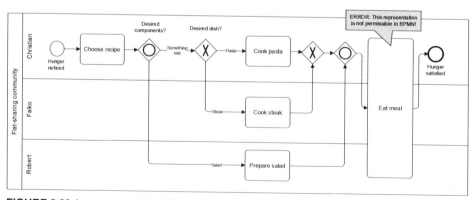

FIGURE 2.26 Incorrect lane handling.

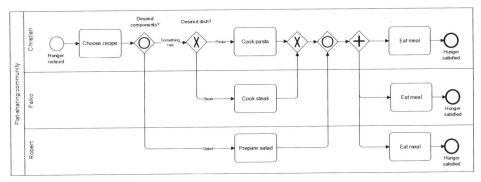

FIGURE 2.27 Correct lane handling.

The solution for keeping Falko and Robert happy is to duplicate the "eat meal" task and to assign this task to each person (figure 2.27). This also makes sense content-wise, because the task actually is completed three times. There is still the possibility of misconception, however, since it is not evident that the three men eat together. It may not matter if Falko and Robert dine with Christian, but in cases where cooperation is intended —perhaps the task is "furnish expert opinion" and you want a joint opinion, not a collection of individual ones —you could apply a group frame as shown in section 2.11.1 on page 80.

Note: In our process diagrams, we don't separate lane captions from the lanes themselves. This complies with BPMN version 2.0, which explicitly forbids such a separation. This is a change from version 1.2, where it was permitted. You may encounter BPMN diagrams like figure 2.28, and the tool you work with may only allow lanes with separate lane headers.

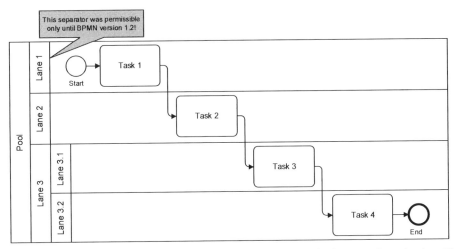

FIGURE 2.28 The lane separators between lane header and lane body were allowed only until BPMN 1.2.

■ 2.6 Events

2.6.1 Relevance in BPMN

Tasks and gateways are two of three flow elements we've come to know so far: Things (tasks) have to be done under certain circumstances (gateways). What flow element is still missing? The things (events) that are supposed to happen. Events are no less important for BPMN process models than tasks or gateways. We should start with some basic principles for applying them. In section 2.2 on page 19, we saw:

- Catching events and throwing events
- Start events, intermediate events, and end events

Catching events are events with a defined trigger. We consider that they take place once the trigger has activated or fired. As an intellectual construct, that is relatively intricate, so we simplify by calling them catching events. The point is that these events influence the course of the process and therefore must be modeled. Catching events may result in:

- The process starting
- The process or a process path continuing
- The task currently processed or the subprocess being canceled
- (As of BPMN 2.0) Another process path being used while a task or a subprocess executes

Throwing events are assumed by BPMN to trigger themselves instead of reacting to a trigger. You could say that they are active compared to passive catching events. We call them throwing events for short, because the process triggers them. Throwing events can be:

- Triggered during the process
- Triggered at the end of the process

Start events are therefore events that always occur. The process cannot trigger an event before it has even started. The simplest application of a start event is shown in figure 2.29. When the event occurs, the process starts.

FIGURE 2.29 Once event 1 occurs, the process is started.

Note: The question mark in the circle indicates that this event can be allocated to a certain type. So far, we have only covered none events. The possible event types are explained in the following sections.

Different events may trigger the process, which could be modeled as shown in figure 2.30 on the next page. It is important that each event triggers its own process instance.

On the other hand, suppose you want to model several events that have to take place before the process starts. A lot of people would model this situation as shown in figure 2.31 on the facing page.

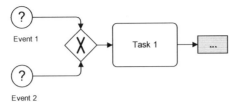

FIGURE 2.30 Once events 1 *or* event 2 occurs, the process is started.

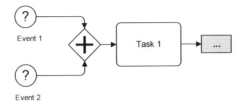

FIGURE 2.31 **Bad**: Technically speaking, this model would lead to a deadlock.

This is intuitive, but unfortunately it is not correct, and few BPMN beginners understand why it is not correct. The reason is that the AND merge does not support the correlation already mentioned in section 2.1.4 on page 18, so the process will not recognize the two events as being associated. We will explain this problem in greater detail in section 2.6.14 on page 51, and we will describe how BPMN provides the solution.

The process may require that a specific **intermediate event** occurs, as shown in figure 2.32. After task 1 completes, event 1 has to occur before task 2 can complete. With the token approach, the token waits at event 1 until it occurs. Only then does the token continue, and it starts task 2.

FIGURE 2.32 After task 1, the process waits until event 1 has occurred. Only then does it proceed to task 2.

Note: The none event (as explained in section 2.2 on page 19) is *not* a catching event. It belongs to the throwing events.

How can we represent that a process has to wait for two events? What we show in figure 2.33 on the next page is flawed. After task 1 completes, the token continues and waits for event 1 to occur. If event 2 occurs while the token is waiting on event 1, the token will not notice it. Even worse, if event 1 occurs after event 2, the token continues and then waits for event 2 to occur. Since event 2 already occurred, the token will wait forever.

The semantics of catching events is therefore *not* to check for a condition that already may have been fulfilled, but to treat the catching event as a transitory signal that vanishes immediately after the occurrence. The process therefore can handle the event only if it waits for the event at exactly the moment it occurs. This "strict explosion semantics," as

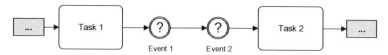

FIGURE 2.33 Sequential intermediate events can only be recognized one after the other.

we call it, can usually be ignored in purely functional process modeling, however, it must be adhered to in technical process modeling (section 5.4.2).

If we need to wait for two events that may occur independently, but both events must occur before the process can continue, we represent the situation as in figure 2.34.

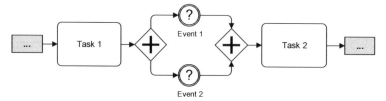

FIGURE 2.34 Using the AND gateway to wait for several events at the same time.

We can model attached intermediate events with BPMN. These do not explicitly require waiting, but they do interrupt our activities, both tasks and subprocesses (which will be discussed later). Such intermediate events are attached because we position them at the boundary of the activity we want to interrupt. A token running through the process shown in figure 2.35 would behave this way:

- The token moves to task 1, which starts accordingly.
- If event 1 occurs while task 1 is being processed, task 1 is immediately canceled, and the token moves through the exception flow to task 3.
- On the other hand, if event 1 does not occur, task 1 will be processed, and the token moves through the regular sequence flow to task 2.
- If event 1 occurs only after task 1 completes, it ceases to matter.

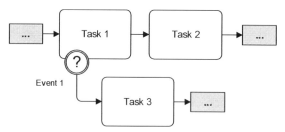

FIGURE 2.35 Event 1 cancels task 1 and starts task 3.

Through BPMN version 1.2, with the exception of compensation events, attached intermediate events inevitably resulted in canceled activities. BPMN 2.0 defines a new symbol: the non-interrupting intermediate event. It sounds awkward, but it is useful. The token moves through the process section shown in figure 2.36 on the facing page as follows:

* The token moves to task 1, which starts accordingly.
* If event 1 occurs while task 1 is being processed, the token is cloned. Task 1 continues to be processed while the second token moves to task 3, which is now also processed. This procedure may even take place repeatedly, that is, the event can occur many times. Each occurrence results in another cloned token.
* If event 1 does *not* occur, task 1 will be completed, and the token moves through the regular sequence flow to task 2.
* If event 1 occurs only after task 1 completes, it ceases to matter.

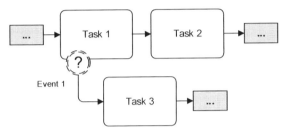

FIGURE 2.36 The occurrence of event 1 results in starting task 3, while task 1 is being further processed.

Throwing intermediate events are triggered by the process. That means a token occurring at such an event triggers it, then immediately moves on. Throwing events do not lead to canceled activities, which is why they can never be attached. They occur only in the sequence flow. We already know the none intermediate event, which can be used to model the entry into a defined status. This is a throwing event too.

In the following sections, we introduce the event types to be used when working with BPMN. We also explain how you can react to different events using the event-based gateway, and the changes that BPMN 2.0 introduces. The event types are:

* Message
* Timer
* Error
* Conditional
* Signal
* Terminate
* Link
* Compensation
* Multiple
* Parallel
* Escalation
* Cancel

2.6.2   Message events

Sooner or later, most processes require communication, which can be represented in BPMN by means of the message event. You'll recognize it as the small envelope. The general application of the message event is shown in figure 2.37.

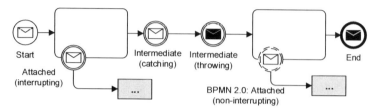

FIGURE 2.37 Applying the message event.

The meaning of "message" in BPMN is not restricted to letters, e-mails, or calls. Any action that refers to a specific addressee and represents or contains information for the addressee is a message. In figure 2.38 for example, the pizza ordering issue has been fully modeled: We choose a pizza, and we order it. We then wait for the pizza to be delivered. After delivery, we eat. Notice that there is no "order pizza" task.

FIGURE 2.38 Ordering and getting pizza as a message event.

What's shown in figure 2.39 would in fact be wrong: The throwing intermediate event "pizza ordered" implies that we have ordered a pizza. If a corresponding task were added, it would result in a double definition and therefore be meaningless.

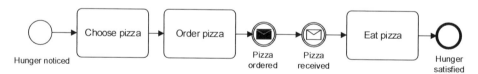

FIGURE 2.39 Wrong content: According to this process model, we would order the pizza twice.

In figure 2.40 on the facing page, we show a message leading to cancellation. In this scenario, we administer a web application. When a user notifies us that the website does not work, we immediately search for the error. But maybe the user is mistaken, and the website is fine. Maybe the user's Internet connection is defective. If the user tells us about the false alarm, we cancel the search and swear at the user for wasting our time. If the error is actually found, however, we eliminate it and simultaneously figure out who caused the error. If the user caused the error, we can swear at the user for a different reason. If the user is not at fault, however, we thank him or her graciously for letting us know about the problem.

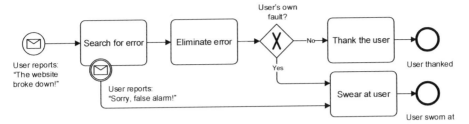

FIGURE 2.40 The attached message event results in the cancellation of the task "Search for error."

Our BPMN Etiquette

We are not always happy with the throwing intermediate event. Implying a "send message" task without modeling it explicitly can easily confuse inexperienced consumers of our models. We choose not to use throwing intermediate events for messages and instead use a task. (See figure 2.41.) In section 2.7 on page 54, we explain that there are special BPMN task types for sending and receiving messages. ∎

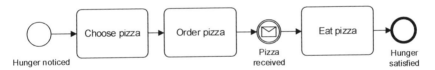

FIGURE 2.41 Our convention: tasks for sending, events for receiving messages.

2.6.3 Timer events

The timer event is often used when working with BPMN because it is so flexible to apply. A clock icon represents the timer event. You can see it applied in figure 2.42. You can use timer events to start processes:

* Once, at a scheduled time
* Repeatedly at scheduled times
* At timed intervals

FIGURE 2.42 Applying a timer event.

- Relative to other events

As an intermediate event, a timer event can stop a process until:

- A scheduled time arrives.
- A defined span of time has elapsed.
- A time relative to another event expires.

Figure 2.43 shows a few examples of applications. Time moves on no matter what we or our processes do, so timer events can exist only as catching starts or intermediate events.

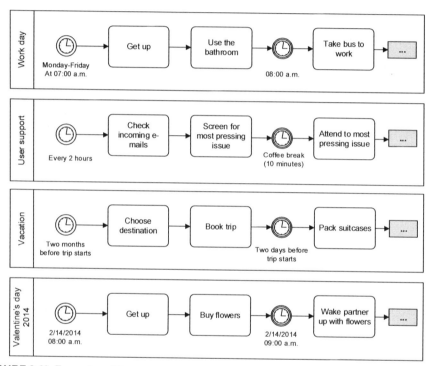

FIGURE 2.43 Examples of timer events.

You can model countdown times with an attached timer event. They are used this way frequently. You can specify upper time limits —the maximum time allowed for a processing task —for instance. Figure 2.44 on the next page shows a process in which a task may take a maximum of 30 minutes. If the time expires before the task completes, the "choose pizza" task is canceled, and we cook pasta instead. In either case, we eat the meal at the end.

Non-interrupting timer events became possible with BPMN 2.0. Figure 2.45 on the facing page shows another example of this. Before we can eat, we have to prepare the meal and set the table, but we only start setting the table 10 minutes before the meal is ready.

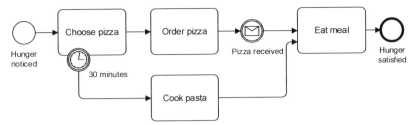

FIGURE 2.44 The timeout for the "choose pizza" task is 30 minutes.

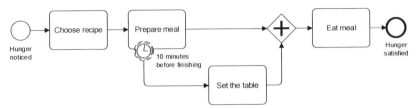

FIGURE 2.45 You can attach timer events that do not lead to cancellation, but instead generate another token.

2.6.4   Error events

Do your processes run completely error-free? If not, you can identify potential errors in your models as a step toward eliminating them, or as part of modeling escalation processes. In BPMN, error events are represented by a flash symbol. Apply them as shown in figure 2.46.

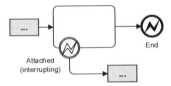

FIGURE 2.46 Applying an error event.

The BPMN specification does not specify what an error may be. As the modeler, you have to decide that. Section 4.5.1 on page 128 has some hands-on tips.

An error is a serious event in BPMN, so it can be modeled only as an attached intermediate event. This means that an error during task execution must be handled in a specific way: As a throwing event, it can be modeled only at the end of a process path so that the participant knows the process has failed. The parent process should likewise recognize the failure. (We explain the interaction between parent and subprocesses in section 2.8 on page 59. You'll also find an example of applying an error event there.)

2.6.5 Conditional

Sometimes we only want a process to start or to continue if a certain condition is true. Anything can be a condition, and conditions are independent of processes, which is why the condition (like the timer event) can only exist as a catching event (figure 2.47).

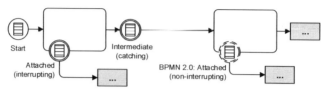

FIGURE 2.47 Applying a conditional event.

We can enhance our pizza process with conditions. If we want to have frozen pizza, the process starts as shown in figure 2.48. We take the pizza from the freezer and turn on the oven. But we only put the pizza in after the temperature in the oven reaches 180 ° C, and we only take it out to eat after it is done.

FIGURE 2.48 Baking pizza under fully modeled conditions.

If we know how long the pizza needs to cook, we can specify this in the process model by substituting a timer event for the last conditional event. The whole thing would then look as shown in figure 2.49.

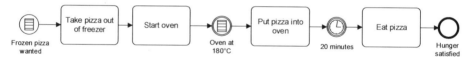

FIGURE 2.49 Baking pizza with indicated baking time.

2.6.6 Signal events

Signals are similar to messages, which is why you can model them in BPMN as events just as you can with messages (figure 2.50 on the facing page). The symbol for a signal is a triangle. The essential difference between a signal and a message is that that latter is always addressed to a specific recipient. (An e-mail contains the e-mail address of the recipient, a call starts with dialing the telephone number, and so on.) In contrast, a signal is more like a newspaper advertisement or a television commercial. It is relatively undirected. Anyone who receives the signal and wants to react may do so.

We saw a new frozen pizza on TV, and we are keen to try it. Figure 2.51 on the next page illustrates this new situation. We buy the pizza, but we keep it in the freezer until we're

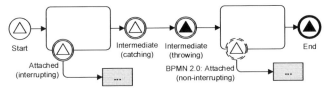

FIGURE 2.50 Applying the signal event.

really hungry for pizza. That's a conditional event. After trying the new pizza, we go to Pizzatest.de to rate the new product. That's a signal. It is a signal for the general public too. (Pizzatest.de actually exists, by the way, which proves again that you can find simply *everything* on the Internet!)

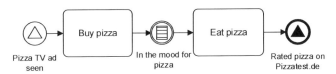

FIGURE 2.51 Pizza signals.

2.6.7 Terminate events

Let's look at the abstract example in figure 2.52. We already discussed (simple) Key Performance Indicator (KPI) analysis in section 2.3.2 on page 22, and we therefore know that this process always takes 55 minutes. After task 1, tasks 2 and 3 can be processed simultaneously. Processing task 2 takes more time than does processing task 3, which is why it determines the runtime of the process. A token that runs through the process is cloned in the AND split. The first token stays in task 2 for 45 minutes; the second token stays in task 3 for 30 minutes. The second token arrives at the none event first, where it is consumed. After 15 more minutes, the first token arrives at the upper none event, where it is consumed too. Since no more tokens are available, the process instance finishes after 55 minutes.

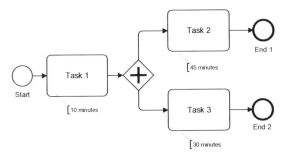

FIGURE 2.52 The process always takes 55 minutes.

So far, so good, but what happens if we already know that, after having completed task 3, task 2 has become redundant? This is a frequent situation with parallel task executions related to content. In such cases, we can apply the pattern shown in figure 2.53.

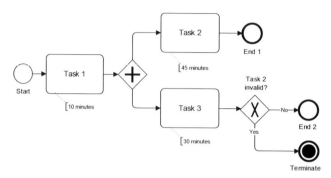

FIGURE 2.53 Potentially, the process terminates immediately after task 3 completes.

We use the terminate event to make sure that *all* available tokens are consumed immediately. That leads to the termination of the process instance, consequently, you can use the terminate event as an end event only. (See figure 2.54.)

FIGURE 2.54 Applying a terminate event.

2.6.8 Link events

The link event is a special case. It has no significance related to content, but it facilitates the diagram-creation process. As shown in figure 2.55, you can draw two associated links as an alternative to a sequence flow. Here, "associated" means there is a throwing link event as the "exit point," and a catching link event as the "entrance point," and the two events are marked as a pair —in our example by the designation "A." Sometimes we use color coding to mark the association.

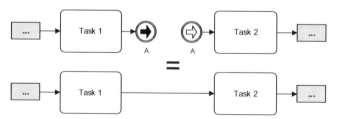

FIGURE 2.55 Associated link events can replace a sequence flow.

Link events can be very useful if:

- You have to distribute a process diagram across several pages. Links orient the reader from one page to the next.
- You draw comprehensive process diagrams with many sequence flows. Links help avoid what otherwise might look like a "spaghetti" diagram.

Link events can be used as intermediate events only (figure 2.56).

Intermediate   Intermediate
(throwing)   (catching)

FIGURE 2.56 Applying a link event.

2.6.9 Compensation events

In practice, we apply compensation icons (see figure 2.57) only to transactions even though BPMN permits other uses. (See section 2.8.5 on page 67.) We execute tasks in our processes that sometimes have to be canceled later under certain circumstances.

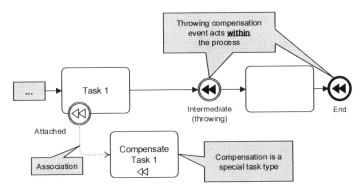

FIGURE 2.57 Applying a compensation event.

Typical examples are:

- Booking a train or airline ticket
- Reserving a rental car
- Charging a credit card
- Commissioning a service provider

In figure 2.58 on the following page, we see this process: On Friday at 1 p.m. we agree with our partner either to go to the theater or to spend the evening with friends. In both cases, we have to do something binding, either to reserve the theater tickets or make the arrangements with our friends. When evening arrives, perhaps we no longer feel like going out at all. We then have to cancel the arrangements we made with the theater or our friends before we can collapse in front of the TV in peace.

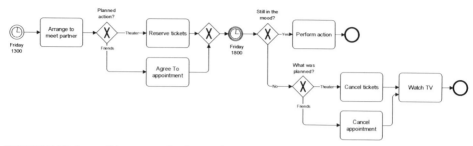

FIGURE 2.58 A possible process for the weekend.

We can represent the latter part of the model more compactly with a compensation event, as shown in figure 2.59. If we don't feel like going out, we have to cancel all our arrangements; we don't have to check which ones to cancel.

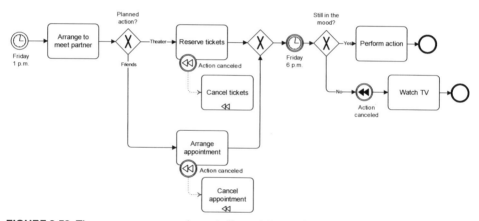

FIGURE 2.59 The same process as shown in figure 2.58, applied to the compensation event.

There are special rules for handling compensations:

▪ Throwing compensations refer to their own processes, so the event is effective within the pool. This shows how this event type differs from a throwing message event.

▪ Other attached events can take effect only while the activities to which they are attached remain active. In contrast, an attached compensation takes effect only if the process triggers a compensation *and* the activity to which the compensation is attached successfully completes.

▪ Attached compensation events connect to compensation tasks through associations, and *not* through sequence flows, which would otherwise be common usage. BPMN thus emphasizes that compensations are beyond the regular process sequence; executing one is an exception.

▪ The obligatory compensation task is a special task type that we explain with other task types in section 2.7 on page 54.

Our BPMN Etiquette

This example may be too simple to illustrate how much work this construct can save you. If you think of the complex business processes that frequently require compensations, however, you'll see how much leaner your models can be. You'll also be quick to spot the circumstances that demand compensations. We use compensation events only occasionally to describe complex processes. ∎

2.6.10 Multiple events

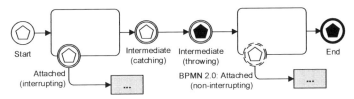

FIGURE 2.60 Application of the multiple event.

We can use the multiple event (figure 2.60) to summarize several events with a single symbol. The semantics are simple:

- If we model the multiple event as a catching event, *only one* of the summarized events has to occur to start or continue the process or to cancel the task.
- If we model a multiple event as a throwing event, it means that *all* of the summarized events are triggered.

Figure 2.61 applies the multiple event to our pizza scenario. In the example, we try a new pizza after having seen it on TV or after a friend recommended it. After eating it, we will rate the pizza on Pizzatest.de and in turn inform our friend if we also recommend this pizza.

FIGURE 2.61 The multiple event summarizes events.

The model in figure 2.62 on the following page describes the same process, but the events are fully modeled.

Our BPMN Etiquette

You have to decide if multiple events serve your purposes. We concede their benefit in rough functional process descriptions, but they cease to be as useful in the

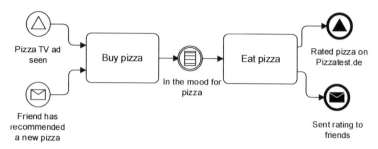

FIGURE 2.62 An alternative for figure 2.61 on the previous page

more advanced technical-implementation phase. You can't afford to leave relevant details hiding in the descriptive text. We don't find the multiple event to be intuitive, nor is it helpful on a functional level. It may make your diagrams larger to model all events separately, but the resulting diagrams will be both more comprehensive and more comprehensible. The bottom line is that we have never used this symbol in practice, nor have we seen anybody else doing so.

2.6.11 Parallel events

The parallel event (see figure 2.63) was added in BPMN 2.0 to supplement the multiple event. While a catching multiple event has XOR semantics —it occurs as soon as *one* of its contained events occurs —the parallel event uses AND semantics. It doesn't occur until *all* of its contained events occur. Because the throwing multiple event already implies AND semantics, the specification defines parallel events as catching events only.

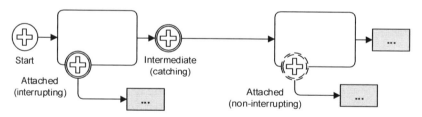

FIGURE 2.63 Application of the parallel event.

2.6.12 Escalation events

The BPMN 2.0 specification added the escalation event (see figure 2.64 on the next page). Mainly, it shows communication between parent and subprocesses. We discuss it in section 2.8 on page 59 with the help of an example.

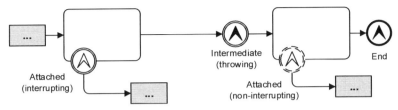

FIGURE 2.64 Applying an escalation event.

2.6.13 Cancel events

You can use the cancel event only in the context of the transactions we discuss in section 2.8.5 on page 67. That section also has examples of applying this event type.

2.6.14 Event-based gateway

We learned about the exclusive data-based (XOR) gateway option in section 2.3.1 on page 20 as a way to use different paths without regard to the data being processed. In figure 2.65, we had to choose a recipe (pasta, steak, or salad) first, and depending on result of the "choose recipe" task, the XOR gateway routed us to the "cook pasta," or "cook steak," or "prepare salad" task accordingly.

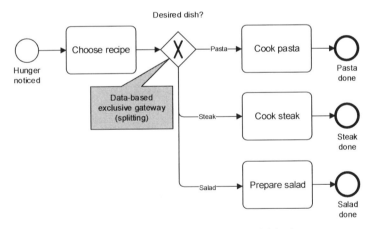

FIGURE 2.65 An XOR gateway decides routing based on available data.

Users of other process notations recognize this type of branching, but BPMN gives us another way to design process paths: the event-based gateway —event gateway, for short. This gateway does not route based on data, but rather by which event takes place next. To understand the benefit, consider the process shown in figure 2.66 on the following page: We order pizza and wait for it to be delivered. We can eat only after we receive the pizza, but what if the pizza doesn't arrive after 60 minutes? We'll make an anxious phone call, that's what! We can model this with the event gateway (figure 2.67 on the next page). Now, in contrast to the data-based XOR split, the token waits at the event gateway for one of the subsequent events to occur. Once any one event occurs, the token takes the respective path. If other events then take place, they are ignored. This is XOR semantics.

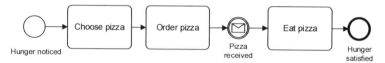

FIGURE 2.66 According to this model, we may wait forever for pizza to be delivered.

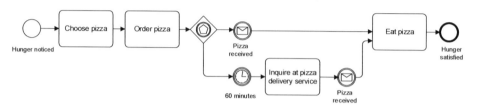

FIGURE 2.67 After the gateway, the path that receives the event first is used.

As you can see in figure 2.68, not all intermediate events combine with the event gateway. You can, however, combine it with the receive task, which we discuss in section 2.7 on page 54.

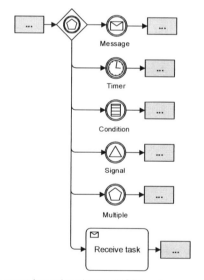

FIGURE 2.68 Applying an event-based exclusive (XOR) gateway.

As an instantiating gateway, the event gateway can be used to start a process. You can combine them with other events to trigger a process and, as shown in figure 2.69 on the facing page, they can be merged through XOR merges.

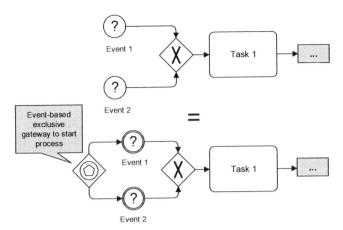

FIGURE 2.69 The event gateway can be a starting point, but it must be of the instantiating type.

 Our BPMN Etiquette

We find it cumbersome and non-intuitive to modeling start events with event gateways. Instead, we use XOR merges without event gateways. ■

2.6.15 Event-based parallel gateway

BPMN 2.0 adds a variation on the event gateway: the event-based parallel gateway. Use of this symbol expresses that all subsequent events have to occur before a process can be started completely. It therefore provides correlation not provided by the simple AND merge.

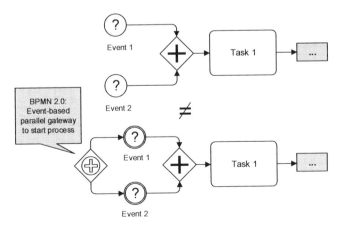

FIGURE 2.70 The lower model works, the upper one (strictly speaking) does not.

The lower model shown in figure 2.70 causes the following behavior:

- If event 1 occurs, the process instance is started and a token is born.
- The new token waits at the AND merge.
- If event 2 occurs, the related process instance already started is identified. (This is correlation.) At event 2, another token is born.
- The second token also moves to the AND merge, where it merges with the first token. Only a single token leaves by the outgoing path.

The *upper* model shows that the allocation to the running process instance would not be carried out. Instead, two isolated instances start in which a token waits forever at each AND merge. This "strict correlation semantics" of BPMN doesn't always further the goal of making process models easy to understand!

■ 2.7   Special tasks

2.7.1   Typification

So far, we have used only tasks of undefined types, though BPMN provides the opportunity to work with task types just as it does for event types. Primarily, task types are intended to model processes that are technically executable. Task types are applied infrequently in practice. We know from experience, however, that task types can be particularly useful when modeling engineering requirements.

Through version 1.2, the BPMN specification did not provide task type symbols, so BPMN tools offered a variety of solutions. You may therefore come across models built on the BPMN 1.2 specification that reflect this deficiency. Our examples use the standard symbols defined by BPMN 2.0.

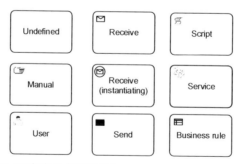

FIGURE 2.71 Task type symbols in BPMN 2.0.

Types of tasks include:

- Manual
- User
- Service
- Receive and send

* Business rule
* Custom

Manual tasks: Tasks executed by a human being that do not affect the completion of a task assigned by the process engine. All the tasks from our various pizza processes are manual types.

Other examples:

* File a document in a folder
* Clarify an incorrect invoice by phone
* Talk with customers at the counter

User tasks: User tasks are executed by people too, but they are assigned by a process engine, which may, for example, place these tasks in each user's task list. After the human finishes a task, the engine expects confirmation, usually including data input or a button click. User tasks are part of the Human Workflow Management.

Typical task examples from the world of Human Workflow Management are:

* Check an invoice
* Approve an application for vacation
* Process a support request

Service tasks: Service tasks are those done by software. These are program functions applied automatically as a process executes. BPMN normally assumes that this function is provided as web service, though it can be another implementation. The service task is a component of process-oriented implementation integration, which explains why it is so similar in concept to Service-Oriented Architecture (SOA).

Typical examples from the world of implementation integration are:

* The credit rating provided by a rating agency, obtained as XML through HTTP during a credit check
* Booking an invoice received as EDIFACT through X.400 in SAP R/3
* The offer of substandard goods by an online auction house, as a web service

Receive and send tasks: Receiving a message can be modeled as a separate task. This task type is an alternative to the catching message event, which is why the symbol for the event defined in BPMN 2.0 is an empty envelope. If a receive task is to instantiate a process, that is, the receive task replaces the message start event, this is shown by a small event symbol in the top left corner. The same principle applies to send tasks. These tasks are technical, and the process engine executes them. Therefore, they mainly are used for calling web services asynchronously through message queues and accepting service requests for asynchronous processing.

Script tasks: Scripts execute directly in the process engine, so they must be written in a language that the process engine can interpret.

Business rule tasks: BPMN 2.0 provides another task type: the business rule. This task type is used solely to apply business rules. We discuss this further in section 4.5.4 on page 135 and section 5.8 on page 176.

Custom task types: You can define your own task types with individual symbols to customize your diagrams and to make them express conditions in your organization better. Your BPMN tool must provide this option, of course. We have yet to encounter anyone who has done this —most people don't even know it's possible. Even so, we can imagine task types for:

* Phone calls
* Signatures
* Approvals or rejections
* Archiving

2.7.2 Markers

In addition to those various types of tasks, we can mark tasks as loops, multiple instances, or compensations. Markers can be combined with the assigned types.

2.7.2.1 Loops

A loop task repeats until a defined condition either applies or ceases to apply. Perhaps we suggest various dishes to our dinner guests until everyone agrees. Then, we can prepare the meal (figure 2.72).

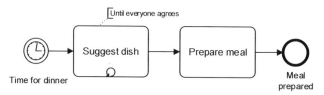

FIGURE 2.72 We keep suggesting dishes until everyone agrees with a suggestion.

Do we absolutely need the loop symbol for this process model? No, we could just model a return with gateways, without gateways, or both. We discussed these methods in section 2.3 on page 20 and section 2.4 on page 30. It becomes a question of which alternative in figure 2.73 on the next page you prefer, because they all are equally correct syntactically, and they are semantically identical to the process shown in figure 2.72. Depending on what you choose (the loop symbol, gateways, or conditional flows), apply it in your models in a standardized way.

In the example, we executed the task first and checked afterwards to see if we needed it to execute again. Programmers know the principle as the "do-while" construct. We can also apply a "while-do" construct, however, and so check for a condition before the task instead of afterward. This occurs rarely, but it makes sense if the task may not execute at all.

You can attach the condition on which a loop task executes for the first time or, as shown in the example, apply the condition on repeated executions as an annotation to the task. You can store this condition as an attribute in a formal language of your BPMN tool as well. That makes sense if the process is to be executed by a process engine, which is why we take up this topic again in section 5.4.4 on page 166.

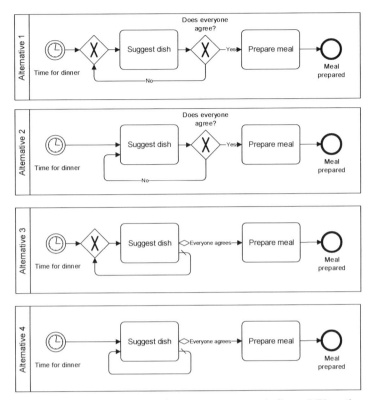

FIGURE 2.73 All four variations represent the same process as in figure 2.72 on the preceding page.

2.7.2.2 Multiple task

The individual cycles of a loop task must follow each other. If for example we live in a flat-sharing community and the roommates feel like eating pizza, the "choose pizza" task must be repeated for each roommate before we can order. You'd sit together and pass a menu around until finally everyone has made a decision. There are student apartments where they *do* handle it like that —more evidence that students have too much time on their hands! It is much more efficient for all roommates to look at the menu at once, and they choose a pizza together. You can model this process using the "multiple task" (figure 2.74). A multiple task instantiates repeatedly and can be executed in sequence or in parallel, with the latter being the more interesting case.

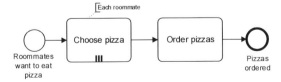

FIGURE 2.74 Using the multiple task to make tasks dynamically parallel.

Do you think the example is absurd? How does your company check invoices for group orders, such as for office supplies? Do you forward the invoice from one employee to the next, so that each person can sign off on the items he or she ordered, before you pay the invoice? If so, you live in a flat-sharing community, and you urgently should consider optimizing your process. Automating invoices is still one of the top BPM projects, and the top goal of such projects often is one of parallelization.

2.7.2.3   Compensation

We explained the benefit of the compensation event in section 2.6.9 on page 47 by means of an example. The compensation task type is applied exclusively in the context of a compensation event. Accordingly, it is integrated in the process diagram only by associations, never by sequence flows.

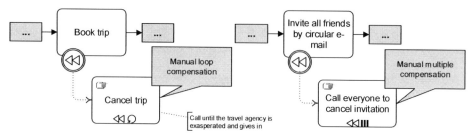

FIGURE 2.75 The compensation and loop/multiple markers can be combined both with each other and with task types.

The possible combination of the compensation with a loop or multiple instance as shown in figure 2.75 is worth mentioning. In this case, both markers are placed in parallel. As with the other markers, the compensation can be combined with the task types already introduced. A manual compensation task that repeats until it succeeds or that executes repeatedly and in parallel as far as possible (figure 2.75), is therefore eminently practical.

2.7.3   Global tasks and call activity

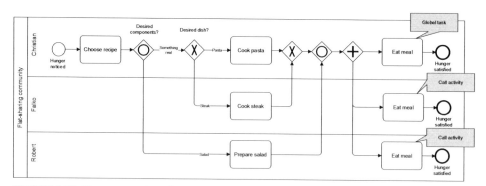

FIGURE 2.76 The process from figure 2.27 on page 35 as it had to be represented in BPMN 2.0.

Since BPMN 2.0, we are able to define global tasks, which differ from the regular tasks in that you can reference them by means of a "call activity." Call activities have a thicker frame than other activities, as the diagram in figure 2.76 on the facing page shows.

2.8 Subprocesses

2.8.1 Encapsulate complexity

The examples in this book either deal with simple processes, or they diagram complex processes superficially so that the models fit on one page. When modeling your process landscape, you don't have this luxury. You have to rough out your processes so that you can get the general ideas in place and recognize correlations. Then you have to develop a detailed description, so that you can analyze exactly where the weak points are or how you'll have to execute the process in practice. The possible top-down refinements or bottom-up aggregations mark the difference between true process models and banal flow charts, between sophisticated BPM software products and mere drawing programs.

BPMN provides us with the subprocess to help with the expanding/collapsing view. A subprocess describes a detailed sequence, but it takes no more space in the diagram of the parent process than does a task. Both tasks and subprocesses are part of the activities class and are therefore represented as rectangles with rounded corners. The only difference is the plus sign, indicating a stored detailed sequence for the subprocess. (See figure 2.77.)

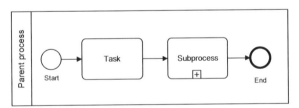

FIGURE 2.77 A task and a subprocess.

What good is that to us? That depends most on how your BPMN tool supports the following options for connecting subprocesses with their parent processes:

- **Representation in a separate process diagram**: The subprocess symbol links to a separate diagram. If your BPMN tool displays the process model in a web browser, for instance, clicking on the symbol would open a new page to display the detail diagram. (See figure 2.78 on the following page.)
- **Expanding in the process diagram of the parent process**: The activity with the plus sign is called a collapsed subprocess. The plus sign suggests that you could click on it and make the subprocess expand. The BPMN specification provides for this option, though not all tool suppliers implement it. Figure 2.79 on the next page shows how the subprocess was directly expanded in the diagram of the parent process. A tool supporting this function enables you to expand and collapse the subprocess directly in the diagram, respectively, to show or hide details.

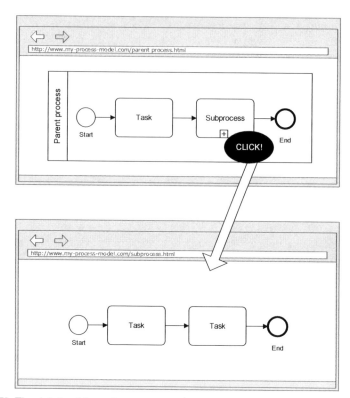

FIGURE 2.78 The details of the subprocess are shown in a separate diagram.

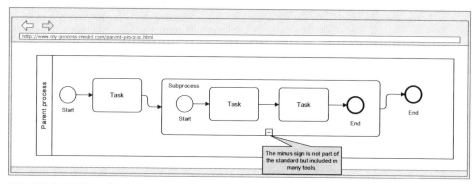

FIGURE 2.79 The subprocess expands directly in the diagram of the parent process.

Direct expansion may seem appealing, but often it is not useful in practice. Expanding the subprocess requires that all the adjacent symbols in the diagram shift to make room. This can result in sluggish performance with a complex diagram, and it can be visually ... nasty. The most important thing is that your tool provides for linking and that you can usefully navigate through the diagrams. In other words, it supports the first option above. Yes, it can be helpful to have your subprocess modeled and expandable directly from the parent process. That means process segments remain localized, and you can attach events too (see section 2.8.3 on page 64). This is, however, the less important option.

The sequence flow of the parent process ends in both cases at the left edge of the subprocess. The next sequence flow starts at the right edge. This means that sequence flows are not allowed to exceed the boundaries of the subprocess, which not every beginner knows, and which becomes a problem when a subprocess expands.

Visualize a token that behaves as follows:

- The parent process starts, and a token is born.
- The token runs through the task and arrives at the subprocess, which causes the parent process to create an instance of the subprocess.
- Within the subprocess, a separate token is born which runs through the subprocess from the start to the end event, but the token of the parent process waits until the subprocess completes.
- When the subprocess token arrives at the end event, it is consumed, which completes the subprocess. Now the token of the parent process moves to its own end event.

The encapsulation in subprocesses that we're describing isn't restricted to two levels. You could just as easily have a parent process as a subprocess, or you could model further subprocesses on the level of a defined subprocess. How many levels you use and the level of detail you apply to model them is up to you. BPMN doesn't specify this, and there can be no cross-company or cross-scenario cookbook to define levels. Participants in our BPMN workshops don't like this, but there's no point in hiding the fact nor attempting to explain it away. In the following chapters, we work often with subprocesses in explaining our best practices, but the truth is the number of refinement levels and their respective levels of detail is always situational. It depends on the organization, the roles of the project participants, and the goals for the process you're modeling.

BPMN also enables you to place the start and end events directly on the boundary of the subprocess (figure 2.80). That works, of course, only if the subprocess is expanded within the parent process. Not many BPMN tools support this method, and we see no specific benefit in it. We therefore cannot recommend it.

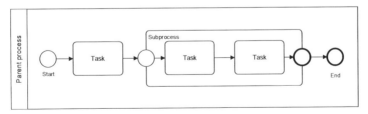

FIGURE 2.80 Start and end events stored directly at the boundary of the subprocess.

You may remember that we explained in section 2.2 on page 19 that you can work without start and end events. Without them, you can make the parallelization shown in the top part of figure 2.81 on the next page somewhat more compact. In this example, start and end events were used in the parent process, but not in the expanded subprocess. That's completely legitimate, but we don't do this ourselves for two reasons:

1. It increases the risk of confusing inexperienced consumers of the model.

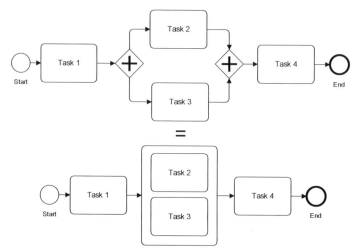

FIGURE 2.81 A subprocess can be used to replace the AND gateways.

2. It is easy to confuse the representation with the ad hoc subprocess to be introduced later in the book. We use that a lot.

The example shows that subprocesses in BPMN practice are used not only to refine processes in terms of content; they are also a "technical stylistic device" for creating diagrams. The following sections illustrate this.

2.8.2 Modularization and reuse

In version 1.2, BPMN differentiated between embedded and reusable subprocesses by assigning an attribute to a subprocess. In version 2.0, BPMN maintains this differentiation in principle, but it is defined differently. A subprocess now is embedded intrinsically, and it can be reused only by defining it as a global subprocess, and then referencing it by means of a call activity. We therefore refer to embedded subprocesses and global subprocesses in the following.

An embedded subprocess can occur only within a parent process to which it belongs. An embedded subprocess cannot contain pools and lanes, but it can be placed within the pool or the lane of the parent process. Furthermore, an embedded subprocess may have only a none start event; start events such as messages or timers are not permitted. An embedded subprocess has essentially nothing more than a kind of delimited scope within the parent process, which may serve two goals:

1. To encapsulate complexity (as already described)
2. To formulate a "collective statement" on a part of the parent process by attaching events or placing markers. We deal with this option later.

On the other hand, global subprocesses may occur in completely different parent processes. There are a great many subprocesses that, in practice, are used over and over. A good example is the procurement of an item because a customer ordered it or you need to re-stock supply. Another example is invoicing because you've delivered or repaired an item as shown in figure 2.82. In the example, notice that call activities differ from regular activities by their considerably thicker borders.

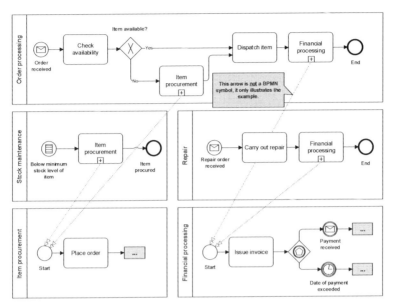

FIGURE 2.82 Examples of reusing subprocesses.

The connection a global subprocesses has to its parent is considerably less close, and they can have their own pools and lanes. You can think of the participant responsible for a subprocess as a service provider for various parent processes. It is a like a shared service center.

The loose connection also affects data transfer between the parent and the subprocess. BPMN assumes that embedded subprocesses can read all the data of the parent process directly, but an explicit assignment is required for global subprocesses to be able to read it. That may seem like merely a technical aspect at first, one that modelers and the consumers of their models care to know about but won't wish to bother with. After some consideration, however, you may see the impact this difference makes on the organization. Consider this: When your accounting department wants to issue an invoice for a repair, it always needs:

* A billing address
* The date of performance delivery
* A description of performance
* An amount to invoice
* An expected date of payment

The owners of order processing, not just the repair department, must provide this data. Accounting will want the data in a standard format, won't it? This corresponds well to what BPMN calls required data mapping between parent processes and global subprocesses. (Do you notice how often these weird techie issues correspond to the organizational needs and expectations of a process?) BPMN simply forces us to formalize

many matters that seem self-evident, or that remained unconscious or forgotten in the
process design. Formalization is our best chance of keeping up in a fast-changing
environment with ever more complex processes.

2.8.3   Attached events

We already learned about intermediate events that can be attached to tasks. The same
events can be attached to subprocesses as well, which opens up a wide range of
opportunity in process modeling. As shown in figure 2.83, we can represent how a
spontaneous dinner invitation leads to canceling our cooking process. In the process
shown, however, we could ignore the invitation if our meal had already been prepared and
we already ate it.

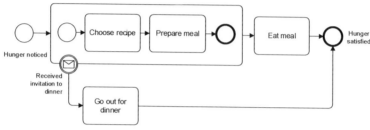

FIGURE 2.83 The catching event cancels the entire subprocess.

Where message, timer, and conditional events are involved, the parent process always
aborts the subprocess when reacting to external circumstances. With error, cancellation,
and escalation events, however, the subprocess reports these events to the parent process.
This isn't as abstract as it may sound.

In the bottom right of figure 2.84 on the facing page, the item procurement task can fail
because the item is no longer available. Because item procurement is a global subprocess,
it triggers an error event to tell the parent process that something went wrong. In business
terms, this may mean that the customer who wanted to buy the item tells a salesperson
that his or her order failed because the item is out of stock. A clerk then orders more of the
item to replenish inventory.

It is interesting that parent processes can handle the error message differently. While the
disappointed customer must be informed within the scope of the order process, it is
sufficient for the stock maintenance process to delete the item from the catalog. The
respective parent processes decide what circumstances require canceling the subprocess
and what happens next. That's a principle that you can use to build flexible and modular
process landscapes.

The signal event serves two functions. A parent process can react to a signal received from
the outside while it executes a subprocess —this is much like a message event. But we also
use the signal event to let the subprocess communicate things other than errors to the
parent process. Primarily, this is because we can't model this type of communication with
message events. BPMN assumes that we always send messages to other participants who
are outside of our pool boundaries; the communication between parent and subprocess

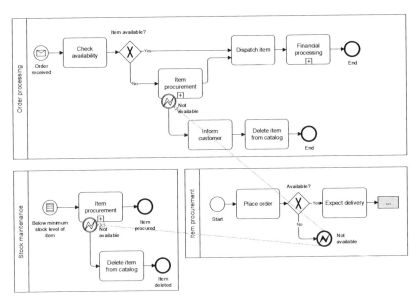

FIGURE 2.84 The subprocess reports an error to its parent.

doesn't fit that mold. We don't use signal events for directed communication, but rather to broadcast information akin to advertisements on the radio.

A better alternative provided in BPMN 2.0 is the escalation event (see figure 2.85).

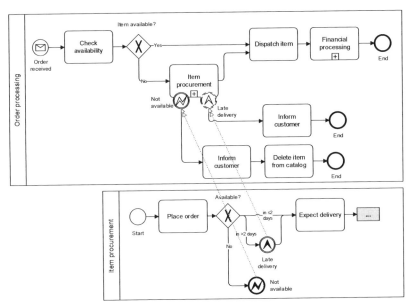

FIGURE 2.85 The escalation event informs the parent process that something needs to be done (available as of BPMN 2.0).

The subprocess can use an escalation event to report directly to the parent process, and the message won't be regarded as an error message. Also, the parent process can receive and process messages from escalation events without canceling the subprocess because non-interrupting intermediate events can be attached .

2.8.4 Markers

You can apply the loop, multiple instance, and compensation task markers that we described in section 2.7.2 on page 56 in a fashion similar to the way you apply subprocesses. You can use them to model even complex loops as shown in figure 2.86. The top and bottom parts of this diagram are equivalent.

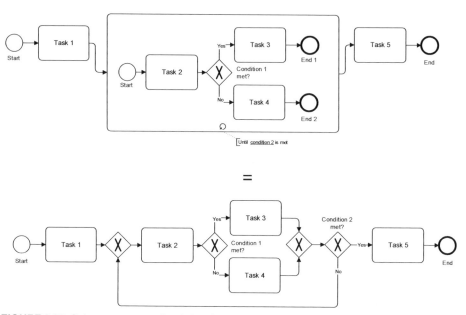

FIGURE 2.86 Subprocesses can be defined as loops.

One marker available only for subprocesses is called ad hoc. Recognize it by the tilde character as shown in (figure 2.87 on the facing page). Use the ad hoc subprocess to mark a segment in which the contained activities (tasks or subprocesses) can be:

* Executed in any order,
* Executed several times, or
* Skipped.

Any party who executes this subprocess decides what to do and when to do it. You could say that the "barely structured" nature of what happens inside this subprocess reduces the whole idea of process modeling to an absurdity because what happens and when are the things we most want to control. On the other hand, this is the reality of many processes, and you can't model them without representing their free-form character. Frequent examples are when a process relies largely on implicit knowledge or creativity, or when

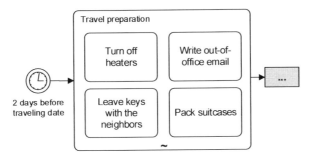

FIGURE 2.87 Travel preparation may include, but does not have to include, these tasks.

different employees carry out a process differently. You can use the ad hoc subprocess to flag what may be an undesirable actual state. Doing so could be a step on the path to a more standardized procedure.

BPMN 2.0 specifies which symbols must, which may, and which are forbidden to occur within an ad hoc subprocess. They are:

* **Must**: Activities
* **May**: Data objects, sequence flows, associations, groups, message flows, gateways, and intermediate events
* **Forbidden**: Start and end events, symbols for conversations and choreographies (discussed later)

By means of the specification, mixed forms —so-called weakly structured processes —can be modeled as shown in figure 2.88.

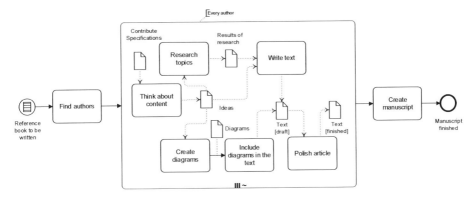

FIGURE 2.88 The processes of the individual authors are not subject to a predefined structure.

2.8.5 Transactions

Many processes work in an all-or-nothing fashion: either all steps must be carried out successfully or nothing must be done at all. The compensation event, which we discussed in section 2.6.9 on page 47, can undo tasks already completed without having to model the undoing in detail. The transaction is a special subprocess, which also helps us in such cases. We explain this in figure 2.89 using the following example:

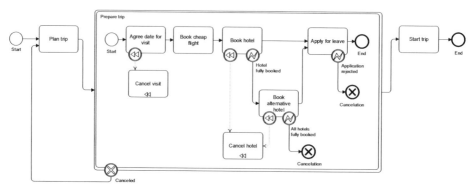

FIGURE 2.89 The double border marks a transaction, in this case the expanded subprocess "travel preparation."

Suppose you want to visit relatives overseas. After deciding to make the trip, you start preparing for it. First, you make a firm plan with your relatives regarding the date and length of your visit. Second, you book a discount flight, and you reserve a hotel room (to avoid being an excessive burden on your hosts, despite their protests to the contrary). Third, you schedule vacation time with your boss. If all goes well, you can start the trip.

What happens, however, if the hotel you wanted is booked and you can't find another? What if the boss denies your vacation request? You have to cancel the travel preparation transaction. The cancel event exists for this purpose. You can only use it within transactions. If you cancel a transaction, it triggers a compensation of all tasks to which corresponding compensation tasks were assigned. You therefore sadly inform your hosts that you won't be able to come at the agreed date, and you cancel the hotel reservation, if any. Because you booked a discount flight, the airline will not refund the ticket price. (You curse them silently.) After compensating for all the tasks already executed, you leave the transaction through the attached cancel event, and you start over with preparations for a different travel plan.

This process is flawed. Because of the cursed airline's poor refund policy, it would make more sense to book the flight only after the other details are confirmed. Book it at the end of, or outside of, the transaction to minimize risk. That's the point: transactions are for critical processes in which even the smallest risk has to be taken into account. If you arrange your vacation time with the boss in advance, the risk of having your request rejected seems small, but it hasn't been reduced to zero, has it? An important bit of work may come in, and your non-binding agreement with the boss may evaporate. Transactions provide security for scenarios like this.

2.8.6   Event subprocesses

BPMN 2.0 introduced a completely new construct, the event subprocess. We locate an event subprocess within another process or subprocess. Recognize them by their dotted-line frames.

A single start event triggers an event subprocess, and this can only happen while the enclosing process or subprocess remains active. For event subprocesses, there can be interrupting (continuous line) and non-interrupting (dashed line) events. This is the same differentiation made as for attached intermediate events. Depending on the type of start event, the event subprocess will cancel the enclosing subprocess, or it will execute simultaneously. You can trigger non-interrupting event subprocesses as often as you wish, as long as the enclosing subprocess remains active.

Okay, that's pretty abstract, but we can demonstrate how an event subprocess works with an example. (See figure 2.90.)

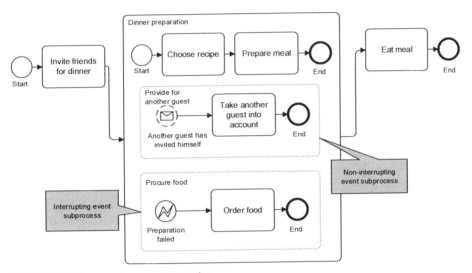

FIGURE 2.90 Event subprocess examples.

We invited a couple of friends for dinner. This starts the "dinner preparation" subprocess of choosing a recipe and then preparing the meal. While we are doing that, the telephone rings. Another guest invites himself to dinner. Spontaneous as we are, we just increase the amount of food or set another place at the table without interrupting the meal preparation. If an accident happens during preparation, however, the error immediately triggers the interrupting event subprocess for remedial action. We order food for delivery. When this event subprocess completes, we exit the enclosing subprocess through the regular exit and attend to eating the meal.

You can see in figure 2.91 on the next page how event subprocesses are represented in collapsed state: The frame is a dotted line, and we have again used the plus sign to represent collapsed subprocesses. In the top left corner, we also have the start event triggering the subprocess.

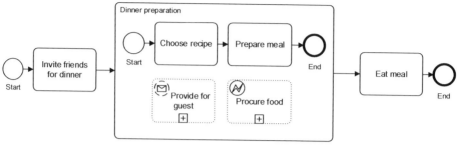

FIGURE 2.91 Collapsed event subprocesses.

The event types that can trigger non-interrupting event subprocesses are:

- Message
- Timer
- Escalation
- Conditional
- Signal
- Multiple
- Multiple parallel

There are two more types for the interrupting event subprocesses:

- Error
- Compensation

Are you wondering if you could model the example without event subprocesses and instead just attach events? Yes, you could. We did it that way in figure 2.92. In terms of sequence, the process works identically to the one shown in figure 2.90 on the preceding page. There is, however, a small but important difference: In the second model, adding an additional guest and ordering the alternative meal do not take place within the "dinner preparation" subprocess, but within the parent process instead. This has the following consequences (which apply particularly to global subprocesses):

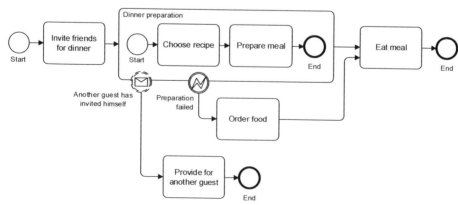

FIGURE 2.92 Compare this process to the one shown in figure 2.90 on the preceding page.

- If responsibility for the subprocess lies with another parent process, two different roles take care of executing the subprocess and handling the related events. If the handling takes place within the subprocess, the same role has to take care of it.
- If the subprocess is global and thus reusable, each parent process must specify how it reacts to both events. On the other hand, if handling takes places within the subprocess, it is reused as well —for good or ill.
- Global subprocesses cannot access directly the data of the top-level process (or their parent processes); some data mapping is required. Data mapping is not required with an event subprocess.

2.9   Pools and message flows

2.9.1   The conductor and the orchestra

In section 2.5 on page 33, we described using lanes to assign responsibility for tasks or subprocesses to different task workers. Lanes always exist in a pool, and the pool boundaries represent process boundaries from start to end. To BPMN, the pool represents a higher-ranking instance compared to its lanes. The pool assumes process control —in other words, it assigns the tasks. It behaves like the conductor of an orchestra, and so this type of process is called "orchestration."

In figure 2.93, the "conductor" arranges for Falko to process task 2 as soon as Robert completes task 1. The conductor has the highest-level control of the process, and each instrument in the orchestra plays the tune the conductor decides upon.

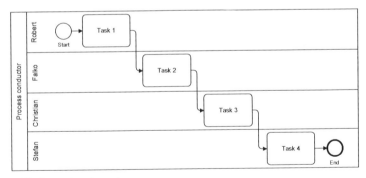

FIGURE 2.93 Tasks and task workers.

Do you think this is unrealistic? Many experienced process modelers have problems with this way of thinking. They would prefer to model a process sequence like that shown in figure 2.94 on the next page on the assumption that no almighty conductor exists in their company, and that individual task workers have to coordinate and cooperate on their own.

To coordinate cooperation with BPMN requires explicit modeling. You assign each task worker a separate pool, and the process passes from one to the next as a message flow (as shown in figure 2.95 on the following page). In principle, this creates four independent

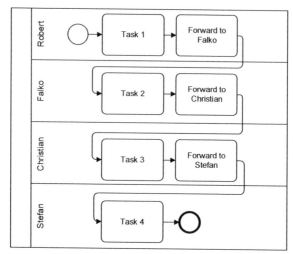

FIGURE 2.94 The task workers provide for the respective successor to start the processing.

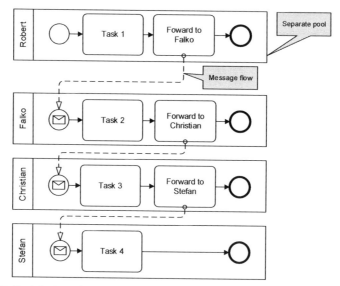

FIGURE 2.95 Each task worker operates in a separate pool.

conductors. These have control over their respective mini-processes, but they can't do anything other than to send messages that trigger their successor processes.

That seems complicated —and you don't have to choose the "coordinated cooperation" method for practical modeling. It reveals a basic principle, however, that you must understand. Even though BPMN lanes look very much like those of other process notations, they represent an entirely different way of thinking, which we attribute to BPMN's origin in the world of process automation. In that world, the process engine controls all tasks in the process, even though different task workers may execute them. So the process engine equates to the mysterious, almighty process conductor.

Have you heard of service orchestration in connection with Service Oriented Architecture (SOA)? That's almost exactly the task of a process engine, except that these services are not only fully automated web services; they also can be tasks executed by human process participants as directed by the process engine. What does that signify, however, for purely functional process modeling, in which you also describe processes *not* controlled by such a process engine? There's no general answer to that question.

You can eliminate pools and work just with lanes, modeling the message exchange as normal tasks as shown in figure 2.94 on the preceding page. That's traditional, and it's a pragmatic solution during, say, a transitional period that allows your co-workers to adapt. In the medium and long terms, however, avoiding pools denies you a powerful device for increasing the significance of process models.

The next chapter explains the most important rules to be observed when working with pools and message flows. Meanwhile, we show the usefulness of this new thinking by example. One thing to remember is that if you strive to harmonize your functional and executable process models to achieve a better alignment of business and IT, you inevitably face this type of process modeling whether you use BPMN or not.

2.9.2 Rules for application

When working with pools and message flows, you may model the following things (see figure 2.96):

- Catching message events, which message flows enter
- Throwing message flows, which message flows exit
- Tasks, which message flows enter *or* exit
- (Expanded) subprocesses, which message flows enter or exit

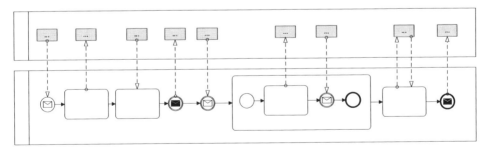

FIGURE 2.96 Acceptable constructs for working with pools and message flows.

The following constructs violate the BPMN specification and therefore must *not* be applied (see figure 2.97 on the next page):

- Sequence flows exceeding pool boundaries
- Message flows *not* exceeding pool boundaries
- Events with message flows that are not of the message type

* Events, which message flows enter *and* exit
* Message flows with arrows at the beginnings and the ends
* Gateways with message flows

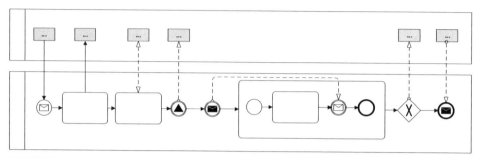

FIGURE 2.97 Forbidden constructs for working with pools and message flows.

2.9.3   The art of collaboration

We examined the process represented in figure 2.98 in connection with the event-based gateway.

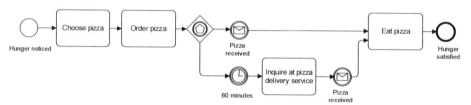

FIGURE 2.98 After the event-based gateway, the path at which the event arrives first is used.

Now consider the broader picture, and think about how this process happens from the point of view of the pizza delivery service. Presumably, it looks like figure 2.99: As soon as we receive an order, we bake the pizza. Our delivery person takes it to the customer and collects the money, whereby the process completes successfully.

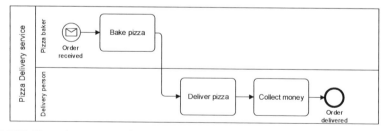

FIGURE 2.99 The sales process of the pizza delivery service.

We want to link the two processes, that is, to examine the interaction of customer and delivery service from a neutral perspective. We can try to model this interaction by means

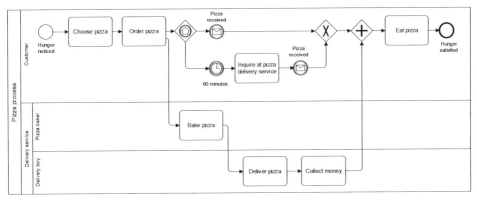

FIGURE 2.100 An overview of the pizza process with one pool and several lanes —a poor solution.

of a pool and lanes as in figure 2.100, but it doesn't work well: There are tasks and events that reference interaction within the pool —waiting for the delivery, for instance, or collecting the money. Other tasks are carried out by roles oblivious to their partners, such as baking the pizza and eating the pizza. It is impossible to differentiate the two visually. Strictly speaking, the diagram is not semantically correct because message events always refer to messages received by the process from outside, and that's not the case here.

If we go with pools, the whole process looks like figure 2.101. Both processes in the combined representation would look just as they did before, but now they connect through message flows. BPMN calls this form of visualization a collaboration diagram. It shows two independent processes collaborating.

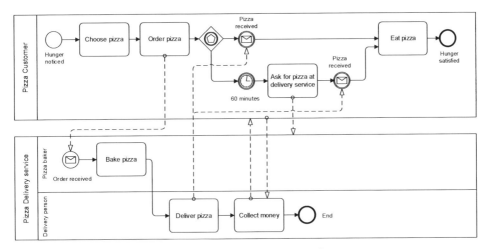

FIGURE 2.101 An overview of the pizza process using two pools.

In two cases, the message flows do not end in an activity or event, but at the participants' respective pool boundaries. The first one comes from the "inquire at delivery service" task; the second one connects to the "collect money" task. The rationale behind the first one is that our inquiry does not influence the sequence flow of the deliverer. The pizza service may provide information or speed up its order processing in anticipation of a new order, but the baking, delivering, and collecting of money doesn't change just because an inquiry came in. As for the "collect money" messages, there's a flaw in the model of the customer process: we have to pay for the pizza *before* we eat it, and that task is still missing. We added it to figure 2.102, and now we can connect the message flows directly to the "pay for pizza" task.

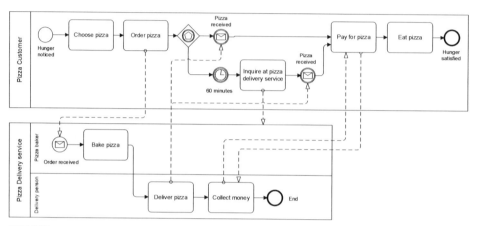

FIGURE 2.102 In the customer's process, the "pay for pizza" task has been added.

2.9.4 Collapse pools

It often happens that we don't know the processes of all parties in detail. We may know the processes of our own company, for example, but not those of a partner company. As long as our partner and we adhere to agreed-upon interfaces, such as receiving or sending certain messages, things can still operate smoothly. As customers of the pizza delivery service, we expect the deliverer to:

* Accept pizza orders,
* Deliver ordered pizzas and collect the money, and
* Be available for inquiries.

As customers, we have little interest in the deliverer's internal process. Maybe he bakes and then delivers the pizza; maybe when he's out of supplies, he gets another pizza service to bake the pizza and deliver it. That's his problem —we simply expect to receive our pizza. In modeling such cases, we can hide the deliverer's process and collapse the pool (see figure 2.103 on the next page).

We could go a step further and collapse the customer's pool too (see figure 2.104 on the facing page). Now we see only the messages to be exchanged, assuming that we label the arrows to give us the general idea. The downside is that we can't recognize interdependencies any more. We can't see if the inquiry always goes out, or only takes place under certain conditions —the actual case. BPMN fixed this problem in version 2.0

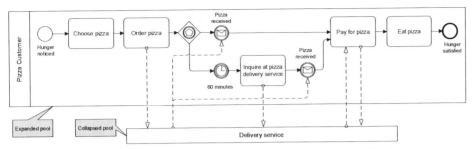

FIGURE 2.103 The deliverer's pool is collapsed, which hides the process details.

by introducing a new type of diagram, the so-called choreography diagram that we describe in section 2.13 on page 87.

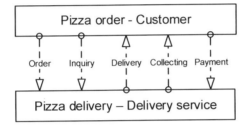

FIGURE 2.104 Both pools are collapsed, and only the message flows are marked.

2.9.5   Multiple instance pools

We showed in section 2.7.2 on page 56 and section 2.8.4 on page 66 that tasks or subprocesses can be marked as multiple, which means that these elements instantiate several times during execution. BPMN 2.0 applies this principle to pools too.

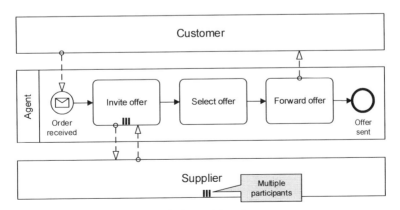

FIGURE 2.105 BPMN 2.0 introduces multiple participants.

Because a pool always represents a participant, we name the construct "multiple participants." Figure 2.105 on the preceding page shows how to apply it. We defined three participants: customer, agent, and supplier. If the agent's process is instantiated, it does so because a customer places an order. This causes the agent to execute the "invite offer" task repeatedly. The supplier pool now has the same marker as the task that executed repeatedly. At a glance, this shows that it is not always the same supplier, but that several suppliers are involved. After obtaining all the offers, one is selected and forwarded to the customer.

The multiple instance participant always helps us when we want to show the interaction of processes in collaboration diagrams. Some processes may instantiate only once while others instantiate several times within the scope of cooperation.

■ 2.10   Data

In the description of a process, BPMN focuses on the sequence flow: the sequence of tasks, gateways, and events. All other potentially relevant aspects to the process execution are treated as less important. The same applies to information or documents used in, or generated by, the process. You can account for these aspects in your diagrams by modeling so-called data objects, which represent all kinds of information regardless of their physical nature. They can include paper documents, abstract information, or electronic data records.

Data objects are coupled to flow objects and sequence flows by means of (data) associations. In addition to their designation, they can be assigned a specific status, which is marked by square brackets in BPMN. Typical statuses for data objects are:

- Generated
- To be checked
- Checked
- To be revised
- Revised
- Rejected
- Approved

The abstract example in figure 2.106 on the next page shows the following interaction of pools 1 and 2: In task 2.1, pool 2 generates the data object 2.1 with the initial status A, which we visualize by means of the directed association from task toward data object. Task 2.3 needs this data object as input, which is why we have drawn another directed association there. Furthermore, task 2.3 consumes the output of task 2.2.

Because these tasks directly follow one another, we can omit the directed associations, and we can connect data object 2.2 directly to the sequence flow. This is just a visual shortcut of the input/output relationship. Task 2.3, in turn, transforms data object 2.1 from status A to status B, and it sends it through a message flow directly to pool 1. (In BPMN 2.0, this situation is no longer visualized by a data object but by a message: an

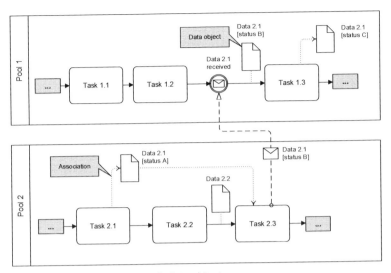

FIGURE 2.106 Examples of working with data objects.

envelope on the message flow.) Pool 1 waits for this message and then forwards the received data 2.1 to task 1.3, where it is transformed from status B to status C.

You have to pay attention when using message flows and directed associations in the same diagram, because they look similar. The most important distinctive features are:

- Message flows are dashed, the beginning of the line is a small circle, and the arrow is a closed triangle.
- Directed associations are dotted, the beginning of the line is unmarked, and the arrow has an open base.

Compared to version 1.2, BPMN 2.0 gives much higher priority to data, and it defines data as an additional category aside from flow objects and artifacts. This promotion was based primarily on the desire to execute BPMN process models directly, and this required more explicit observance of data. For collaboration diagrams, BPMN 2.0 introduced a couple of other new symbols besides the message object. We have applied them to the deliverer's pizza process in figure 2.107 on the following page.

Any new pizza order that the deliverer receives serves as input for the process. Recognize this as the arrow in the top left of the diagram. The order may include one or more pizzas (as expressed by the usual symbol for multiple instances), and the "bake pizza" task must execute a corresponding number of times. The number of instances also corresponds to the number of items in the **collection input data object**. The "collect money" task requires the object for the delivery person to ask for the correct amount. The accountant enters the sale in a journal. This sale is the output of the process, recognizable by the black arrow. The journal is a **data store** that exists, unlike the data objects, regardless of the specific process instance. The journal remains available long after the process instance has ended. If the pizza company was more up to date, its accountant could use software or a database.

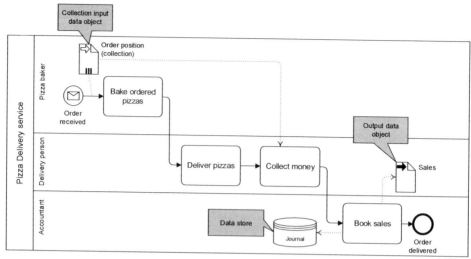

FIGURE 2.107 New symbols in BPMN 2.0.

■ 2.11 Artifacts

2.11.1 Annotations and groups

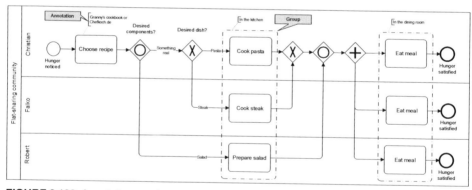

FIGURE 2.108 Annotations and groups.

We use annotations to supplement our diagrams. Annotations can contain almost anything you find useful, and you can connect them to other elements with associations. Usually, we use annotations to provide insight on the execution of tasks (see figure 2.108). (In figure 2.7 on page 23, we used annotations to record the average processing times; in figure 2.72 on page 56, we used them to explain what condition cancels a looping task.)

In figure 2.108, we noted that the food is to be prepared in the kitchen but eaten in the dining room. Because this information refers to several elements in the diagram at the same time, we can group them. Like all artifacts, groups do not influence execution semantics, so don't confuse them with things like subprocesses. You can apply groups any way you like —even across pool boundaries. Groups can be extremely useful for marking off parts of your models to which only certain conventions apply. We will return to this possibility in subsequent chapters.

2.11.2   Custom artifacts

BPMN allows you to introduce symbols that suit your own modeling conventions and particular information needs. In figure 2.109, we expanded the process of delivering pizzas with a bicycle and a computer. These appliances help us execute tasks. Apply the same rules to custom symbols as to all artifacts: connect them with associations to any flow object; place them in any position in the diagram.

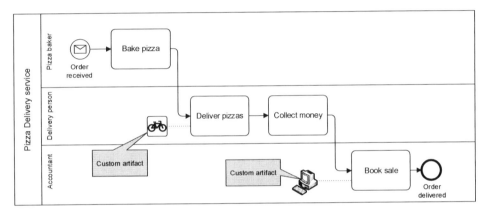

FIGURE 2.109 Applying custom artifacts.

 BPMN-Tooling

You can use custom artifacts only if your BPMN tool supports them. Relatively few products do, unfortunately.

■ 2.12   Comparison with other notations

Many people interested in BPMN already know other process modeling notations. They wonder if switching is worthwhile and what they have to watch out for. In this section, we compare four other notation systems —the ones we encounter most often in our practice —with BPMN. The primary weakness in all of them, which leads us to prefer BPMN, is that they lack the ability to model the interactions of participants acting autonomously. As we saw earlier, simple swimlane representations are insufficient for modeling collaboration. A secondary reason to prefer BPMN is the greater precision it provides, compared to the other notation systems, for handling events.

2.12.1   Extended event-driven process chain (eEPC)

The event-driven process chain (EPC) is a component of the ARIS methodology developed at Saarland University in cooperation with SAP AG. The resulting BPM software, ARIS Toolset, integrated tightly with the ERP (enterprise resource planning) solutions by SAP. Processes implemented in SAP products consequently were documented as EPCs, and that's a major reason they've been implemented so widely. It also made EPC dominant as a notation until 2008. Now, however, it has become apparent that EPC will be superseded by BPMN. Many EPC process modelers are preparing to switch, although that's not always easy because of differences in the approach. Meanwhile, ARIS offers process modeling with BPMN as well.

The EPC consists of the three basic symbols: function, event, and connector. Similar to gateways in BPMN, connectors can function as exclusive branches (XOR), and/or branches (OR), or in parallel (AND). The difference between data- and event-based branches does not exist in EPC. The extended version added symbols to describe organizational units, data, and application systems. You can reference subprocesses through so-called process paths or process signposts.

Converting EPC process models into BPMN is comparatively simple, as shown in figure 2.110 on the facing page, though you need to be careful when converting events. EPC interprets possible data states the same way as it interprets events —incoming messages that trigger a process, for example. You mustn't model data-based decisions as event-based gateways, but rather as data-based gateways. Given EPC's name, it is ironic that BPMN is superior for modeling events. EPC neither differentiates between start, end, or intermediate events nor does it recognize different types such as message or timer. EPC doesn't let you attach events, so it is difficult or impossible to model monitoring functions, troubleshooting, or escalations. Another advantage of BPMN is in how it lets you treat an application as a data object: we could have attached our application as an input to the "check application" task (as in EPC), but instead, we attached it to the sequence flow between the start event and the task. You can thus see at a glance that the document was not already available in the company, but that it was sent there.

EPC still has lots of users. They have a history with EPC, they are used to working with it, and they may find it hard to internalize the new paradigm that BPMN represents. Given the shortcomings of EPC for modeling process automation, however, you should not consider it for modern BPM projects.

2.12.2   UML activity diagram

The activity diagram is one of 13 diagram types defined in UML (Unified Modeling Language) version 2. Like BPMN, UML is managed by the OMG (Object Management Group), though only since 1997. No one should mistake BPMN as a successor to UML, because UML is a general language for modeling software systems. Though it was not developed for modeling business processes, UML activity diagrams have been used often for process modeling —especially for IT projects. One frequent use has been to diagram target state processes as part of developing engineering requirements for new software.

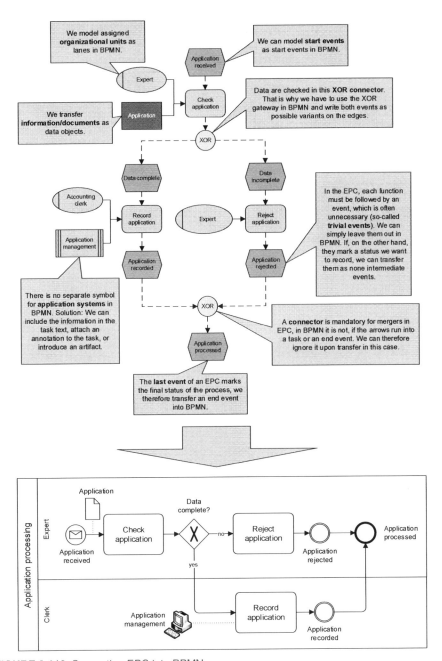

We model assigned **organizational units** as lanes in BPMN.

We can model **start events** as start events in BPMN.

We transfer **information/documents** as data objects.

Data are checked in this **XOR connector**. That is why we have to use the XOR gateway in BPMN and write both events as possible variants on the edges.

In the EPC, each function must be followed by an event, which is often unnecessary (so-called **trivial events**). We can simply leave them out in BPMN. If, on the other hand, they mark a status we want to record, we can transfer them as none intermediate events.

There is no separate symbol for **application systems** in BPMN. Solution: We can include the information in the task text, attach an annotation to the task, or introduce an artifact.

A **connector** is mandatory for mergers in EPC, in BPMN it is not, if the arrows run into a task or an end event. We can therefore ignore it upon transfer in this case.

The **last event** of an EPC marks the final status of the process, we therefore transfer an end event into BPMN.

FIGURE 2.110 Converting EPC into BPMN.

UML's notation for activity diagrams is more comprehensive than EPC's. It contains a couple of symbols specific to software that have no direct equivalent in BPMN, including processing objects and object parameters in individual actions. Most of the current UML symbols for modeling business processes can be converted with no problem. What does become difficult is if you work with interruptible activity regions that cross several lanes. It would be a tidy solution to transfer these into BPMN as embedded subprocesses, but we can't do that because subprocesses in BPMN must not cross lane boundaries. The only solution is to define the subprocesses as global (and thus reusable), and to model the pool and lanes. That may be ugly, but it is the only way to make it work. (See figure 2.111 on the next page.)

Activity diagrams remain important for specifying software-related detailed sequences. Their integration in the UML framework supports this, as does the standardization by the OMG. But we think BPMN is still better for requirements engineering of process-driven applications, particularly if you also need to document process functions. Defining processes that the process engine executes directly is BPMN's specialty. No other notation can match it.

2.12.3   ibo sequence plan

The ibo sequence plan is implemented in Prometheus, which is BPM software from ibo Software. Like EPC, Prometheus is a proprietary notation system. We include it here because it is based on the conventional and widespread flow diagram. (ibo is a management consulting agency with more than 25 years of experience. Most of its customers are from the German-speaking financial world.) Though the ibo sequence plan is well established among process managers, ibo has discovered the advantages of BPMN. It has integrated BPMN into Prometheus.

Most of the symbols of the sequence plan transfer easily into BPMN, as we illustrate in figure 2.112 on page 86. The only problem is when you have a temporal interruption in your sequence plan. This can only be modeled as a timer event if it is caused by a process owner who deliberately does nothing for a certain period, and who then continues the process. We already examined sequences in which an interruption served as an indicator. We *could* continue the process after a countdown expired and because something else needed to happen. That does not work in BPMN. The only solution is to model the event that we're waiting on as a type (a message or a condition, perhaps), and to append an annotation to show how long it usually takes for the event to occur. That gives us a clean control flow without losing the indicator for the average wait time.

2.12.4   Key figures and probabilities

Can BPMN analyze and simulate processes? People who have worked with other notation systems ask this regularly, but the answer may not be a matter of methods but one of tools. What BPM software do you use? Does it let you store key figures and probabilities as well as the corresponding analysis?

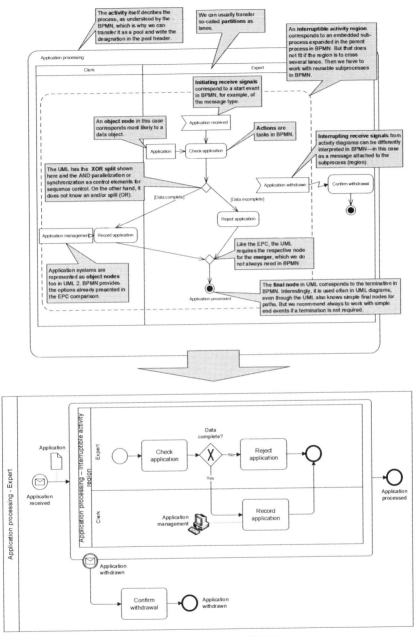

FIGURE 2.111 Converting a UML activity diagram into BPMN.

To be honest, the BPMN specification —even at version 2.0 —does not provide attributes to integrate key figures in process analysis. You could regard that as a regrettable deficit in the standard. On the other hand, simulation is particularly complex, and few people or organizations are willing to spend the time and money to implement it consistently. If the

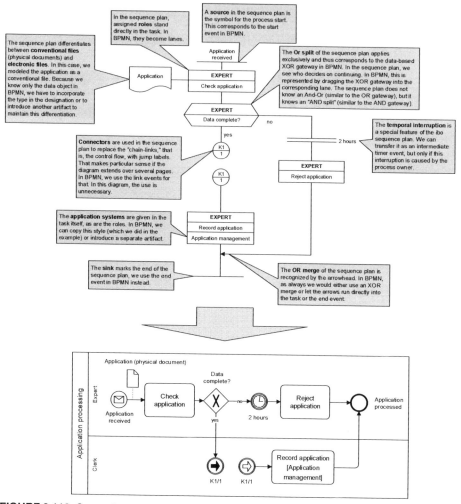

FIGURE 2.112 Converting an ibo sequence plan into BPMN.

BPMN specification represented all aspects of process simulation, the document would probably be 50 to 100 pages longer than it is. The shift in focus might even undermine BPMN in terms of the things it does well.

Figure 2.113 on the next page shows how the key figures lead time (LT), idle time (IT), and cycle time (CT) can be visualized in a process diagram along with probable outcomes. After an application arrives, it sits for about two hours before it is checked. The check takes 15 minutes, then the expert decides whether to reject or record it. Nine times out of ten, the application is recorded. We have modeled possible intermediate states, and we can offer the first analysis: The processing time from receipt to recording is 160 minutes. Rejects take only 140 minutes because the process bypasses the holding time on the clerk's desk. Taking all probabilities into consideration, we know that the average running time for the process is 158 minutes. Appropriately, we note this at the end event.

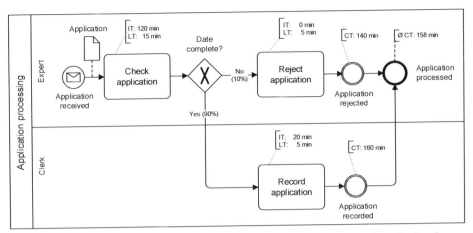

FIGURE 2.113 Possible representation of key figures in BPMN highlighting how the key figures, lead time (LT), idle time (IT), and cycle time (CT), can be visualized.

This is merely one example. Different BPMN tools offer different ways to define key figures, and they provide a variety of ways to depict and to use them. The extent to which process simulation is carried out makes further demands on the process model. Further dependencies may include the occurrence probability of multiple, the capacity of resources, and so on.

■ 2.13   Choreographies and conversations

We showed in section 2.9 on page 71 that BPMN attaches particular importance to the interaction of different participants. BPMN 2.0 describes two completely new modeling methods for this. We have so far seen little value in these methods for real-life projects, but we'll explain their potential. At the bottom right of figure 2.114 on the next page is our pizza collaboration from section 2.9 on page 71. It was merely decorated with the message objects (the envelopes) that were added in BPMN 2.0, and we have positioned them on the message flows.

In the middle of the picture, notice the corresponding **choreography diagram**. This diagram reduces our view of the process to the exchange of messages between participants. In section 2.9.4 on page 76, the pools of both participants were collapsed. Choreography diagrams are considerably more accurate because we can still recognize the fundamental sequence. In the earlier diagram, it appeared that the customer only asked for delivery if 60 minutes elapsed since his or her order. That would be strange. In contrast, a choreography diagram models only the tasks that are relevant to the message exchange, and they do it only once for both participants. This makes the diagram much clearer. The sending participant has a white background; the receiving or reacting participant has a gray background. It does not matter if you place the participants above or below the task. Choreography diagrams can also define subprocesses to be modeled as choreographies.

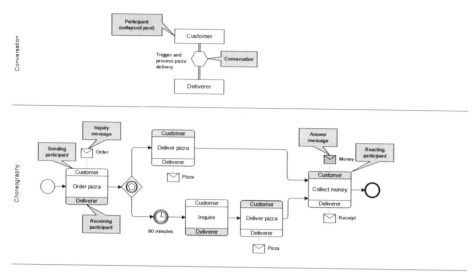

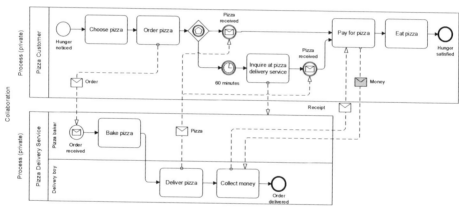

FIGURE 2.114 The pizza story as conversation, choreography, and collaboration.

The top part of the figure models the content of a matching **conversation**. This is the most compact way to represent the participants and their collaboration. A conversation in this regard stands for messages that are exchanged and logically connected to each other. In other words, they correlate. In most cases, a conversation should stand for one collaborative process only. To be precise, we note that conversations in BPMN 2.0 are not a separate type of diagram, but a variant of a collaboration diagram.

When do such diagrams make sense? Some BPMN experts regard them as superfluous, but we disagree. A one-person business may have little need for process modeling, but the systematic examination of processes —from an organizational *or* a technological perspective —only becomes more important as an organization grows larger and more heterogeneous.

As the number of people collaborating in a process increases, the less you can depend on implicit understandings and coordination among them, and the more important process modeling becomes. The same applies even more clearly to process implementation beyond the limits of IT systems. Both choreography diagrams and conversations can represent useful maps for situations where you have to recognize quickly the critical points in a collaboration. If required, you can then model them in more detailed collaboration diagrams.

3

Strategic process models

3.1 About this chapter

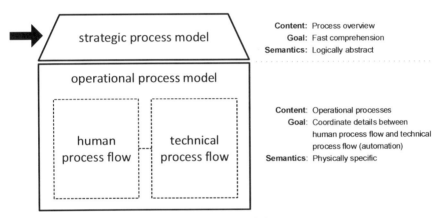

Content: Process overview
Goal: Fast comprehension
Semantics: Logically abstract

Content: Operational processes
Goal: Coordinate details between human process flow and technical process flow (automation)
Semantics: Physically specific

FIGURE 3.1 Strategic process models in the camunda house

3.1.1 Purpose and benefit

You must be able to depict a process from start to end at the strategic level. Such strategic process models are necessarily rough. They are necessarily compact. The audience to bear in mind is likely to be the executive in charge of a company division. He or she may be a process manager or a process owner. The strategic process model also serves process participants, analysts, engineers, and external partners. Yes, these other audiences will need —and they are likely to *insist* upon —more detail, but they also need to have the strategic view if they are to work together toward a goal that makes sense for the organization.

To be readily comprehensible, your strategic diagrams may need to include information on computer systems or human tasks, but the diagrams must remain compact. The point at this stage is to create something that everyone can grasp, and, at a glance, know what the process does, for whom it is done, and the basic sequence of how it gets done.

Consider a strategic model when needs like these exist:

- To clarify what is and is not part of a process.
- To identify resources for a process and assign responsibilities.
- To identify key performance indicators and specify their characteristics. An example KPI may be that a process has a maximum run time of 24 hours.
- To review a process initially in the course of an improvement action.

3.1.2 Model requirements

The chief requirement of a strategic process model is that it is easy to understand —even for people with no experience in BPMN. The model must be comprehensible so that it will be accepted as a means for helping the situation. The title of Steve Krug's book on web usability is wonderfully suggestive when it comes to strategic process models:

Don't Make Me Think!

It also must be abundantly clear who the customer of the process is. Process management philosophy is that a process exists only for carrying out a defined task for a defined customer. Ensuring customer satisfaction is the purpose that defines many performance characteristics, and these characteristics are often the focus for improvement projects.

No one can grasp a process at a glance if the model extends across several pages. Our standard for a strategic model is to fit it onto a single sheet of standard-sized office paper. Orient the paper horizontally, and you automatically have something compatible with PowerPoint. It doesn't help to squeeze in as many lines and boxes as possible. For our strategic models, we limit ourselves to 10 or fewer flow objects and not more than eight artifacts.

In the purposefully plain model we're describing, you can't use the whole array of BPMN symbols. (This isn't the time for compensation events or multiple-instance tasks in any case.) Does the model lose some of its expressiveness? Sure. Does it become less precise? Not necessarily, though it does make for a less granular representation than you might otherwise prefer. Limiting yourself to ten flow objects and eight artifacts is very restrictive too, although you can choose which symbols to use and which to set aside for the sake of simplicity. You can even use custom symbols as artifacts. We'll discuss custom symbols later in this chapter; meanwhile, section 3.3 on page 96 presents a set of symbols that we find useful for strategic diagrams.

The second compromise is a semantic one. In section 3.2 on page 95, we give an example that shows how the semantics of strategic process models cannot be fully consistent. We struggled with this at first, but what we finally came to accept was that insisting on consistent semantics in strategic process models just made the models too complicated. The complexity interfered with the understanding and acceptance we needed from our target audiences, and so the models failed. Now, we knowingly accept inconsistencies, but *only* at the strategic level, mind you!

We remain strict with syntax, however, and we make certain our strategic models are syntactically correct. (The available BPMN tools check syntax and so help to enforce correct syntax anyway.) As a rare exception, we admittedly diverge from the BPMN syntax, but only if the divergence is minor in nature, permitted by the tool, and offers a clear advantage in creating understanding.

 Our BPMN Etiquette

The principle for strategic process models is: Make the syntax as correct as possible, but allow inconsistent semantics if necessary. ∎

3.1.3 Procedure

When do we model strategic processes? We do it either after the initial process discovery, when we have a general idea of an existing process, or at the beginning of process design, when we are configuring the new or improved process (see figure 3.2).

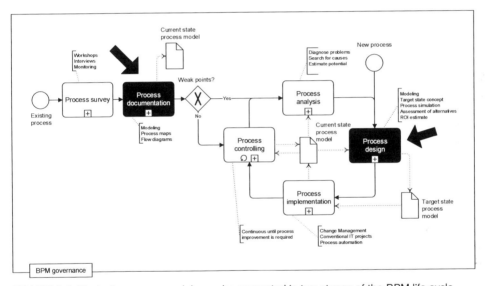

FIGURE 3.2 Strategic process models can be generated in two stages of the BPM life cycle.

It is significantly harder to do an initial discovery of a process than most people think. Sometimes you have documents such as standard operating procedures available, but most of the time you have to interview the process participants or the process managers. These may be one-on-one interviews or group interviews carried out as part of a workshop.

The advantages of a workshop are that you can gain several perspectives at once, and that the participants start feeling invested in the BPM project early on. That can increase acceptance. Workshops can be exhausting, however, because everyone perceives the process differently, because they all want to have their pet variations and contingencies considered, and because they already know what goes wrong. When different departments or teams participate —usually the case because of the comprehensive nature of the processes —discussion can quickly devolve into political squabbling. By then, you stand little chance of creating a differentiated process model. Imagine you've drawn only two rectangles when you hear the first interjections:

- "Before we can confirm the delivery date, we have to check the order details for completeness."
- "But we don't always do that after the order was received! Sometimes we have to check the customer's credit first."
- "But only if the contract volume exceeds 300,000!"
- "And if it is not a class A customer!"
- "Yes, right, that would have to be checked too then. Who takes care of that?"
- "The account executive."
- "In our department, his assistant does. At least, if the account executive is busy."
- "Seriously? Do they even permit that? In our department, he always gives the account executive the order so she can check it!"

And so on. Every BPM expert knows that his or her attempt to get a bird's eye view of the process gets lost in the croaking of the frogs who, naturally, have only a frog perspective. Unless you chair the workshop with an iron fist, the disaster takes its course: Everybody either gives up in exasperation or, even worse, agrees on a process model that looks complete but isn't, one that may even be wrong. You may as well give up too, since your process model will only gather dust in some little-used cabinet!

When you chair an initial survey workshop, use the following as a mantra:

All process models are incomplete —but some of them are useful!

We credit statistician George E. P. Box for inspiring this thought. What it means is that you should *never* attempt to model a process in a greenfield approach, to try to account for every contingency and any possible variation. It simply will not work out. Instead, you should communicate at the beginning of the workshop that you want to start with just a general idea of the process. Set the following goals for this first iteration:

- We want to record the process from start to end.
- We want to record the process in a maximum of eight steps.
- We want to record the standard procedure only.
- We want to record the regular responsibilities.
- We want to record neither the weak points nor to devise improvements.

If you set these goals at the beginning of the workshop, you and your frogs can achieve the first-iteration bird's eye view you need, and you can do it in a span of 30 to 45 minutes! You must be careful to stay on target, however. Whenever a frog tries to escape back to the swamp, you have to stop him!

This first iteration is important psychologically. When it's done, the group will feel a flush of success, and they will see that the process can be managed after all. From this basis, you can launch into the gritty details of the process in subsequent iterations.

Can we start using BPMN in the first iteration? It isn't necessary, but yes, we can, and doing so has a benefit: It gives the group a good initial feel for the symbols and practices. You can also use index cards. For some time now, we have been experimenting with BPMN symbols attached to a white board with magnets. You can move them around easily during the discussion.

■ 3.2   Case example: Recruiting process

Robert, a Human Resources manager, wants to improve the recruiting process. He believes that his staff members do too many tasks by hand that could be handled more efficiently by software. Moreover, he's tired of hearing complaints from other departments about how long it takes to fill vacancies.

Robert is convinced that most of the delays are because the managers of those other departments spend too much time vetting candidates. Also, they don't provide enough information with their requisitions, and they are slow to respond to questions. He can't prove his suspicions though.

Talking with us, Robert describes the recruiting process:

"When a department wants to fill a vacancy, the manager notifies me by e-mail. They fill out a form —it's just an Excel spreadsheet —where they enter the job title, and a job description, and their requirements, and..."

We interrupt Robert. The point, we explain, is not to discuss the cells in his Excel spreadsheet. We are interested in the basic sequence. The other stuff comes later.

"Oh, okay. So they notify me of the vacancy by e-mail. I have to check to whom I forward the e-mail, and that depends on who's available at that moment. Usually I just ask around, since we are all in one office anyway."

Again, we have to dampen Robert's talkativeness. Patiently, we explain that the point is merely to record the most important process steps and to set aside any operational details. He seems taken aback, but he continues:

"Well, then it's simple: We post the job and wait for appropriate applications. We check the applications, select a candidate, and fill the position. Essentially, our job is done if the selected candidate signs an employment contract, even though we have to yet record his or her information in the personnel files. Is this still too much detail?"

It is. For us, however, we can now extract the following key data about Robert's process:

- The process is triggered by a department's requirement to fill a vacancy.
- A job is posted, applicants apply, applications are checked, and the vacancy is filled.
- The process has reached its target when the vacancy is filled, in other words, when an employment contract is signed.

Based on the key data, we build the process model in figure 3.3 on the next page, which Robert understands right away, although we did have to explain a little about the conditional event that triggers the process. We deliberately put the end event in the department's lane to follow the BPM principle of starting and ending processes with the customer.

As a BPMN adept, did the semantic inconsistency of the model catch your eye? If we imagine a token running through the process, we have a huge problem with the "submit application" task and also the "check applications" task. If a single application was submitted, it is impossible to check several applications. That is a contradiction in content, a semantic inconsistency.

The problem doesn't get better by changing the task description to the plural form "submit applications." That makes it look as though one applicant applied for the job

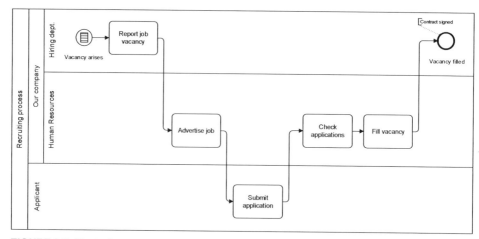

FIGURE 3.3 Strategic process model for the recruiting process.

repeatedly, and that's probably nonsense too. The truth is that there is no formal, clear, syntactically correct solution for this, assuming that we want the model to remain as easy to understand as it is now.

What does Robert say about our problem? Probably nothing. For him, the connection between these tasks is obvious, and he grasps the basic sequence of the process at a glance. We have achieved what we needed from the strategic process model, so we smile and nod and keep quiet about the semantic inconsistency.

The representation has another shortcoming: You can't tell from the diagram that examining the job applications involves the requesting department as well as Human Resources. We accept this inaccuracy at the strategic level as well, since we haven't started the detailed analysis phase yet. If we model a task or a subprocess involving more than one process participant, we assign the activity to the lane of the party responsible for successful completion.

◼ 3.3   Restricting the symbol set

As we showed in Chapter 2, BPMN has more than 50 symbols. That's far too many for strategic process models, and it is why we use only a subset of symbols. Use any subset you choose for strategic process models, but our suggestions follow.

3.3.1   Pools and lanes

After reading section 2.9 on page 71, you should assess figure 3.3 critically. After all, BPMN requires a conductor for each process, one who orchestrates (assigns tasks to) all the people and systems in the process. But this process isn't controlled by a process engine, so there is no conductor here. When the requesting department sends its request to Human

Resources, there is no forwarding of the instance, so you should model it as a message flow. Also, you should assign the requesting department to another pool.

In figure 3.4, we did assign the requesting department to another pool. It now reports its vacancy explicitly in the form of a message to HR and, if the vacancy can be filled, the requesting department is informed likewise.

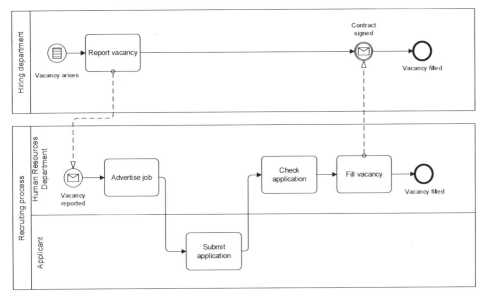

FIGURE 3.4 Reassigning the requesting department to a separate pool.

While this representation has its charm, a problem still exists: The applicants are not orchestrated by a conductor either. (A conductor for this pool would have equal control over both applicants and HR.) Figure 3.5 on the next page shows the collaboration when each party has its own pool.

The more we detail our model of the collaboration, the more questions arise, and the more we can detect inaccuracies and inconsistencies. How does an applicant learn about the vacancy? If he or she responds to a published notice, we should model this with a signal event, not a message. And the diagram still shows that we are waiting for one application instead of several, nor is it clear that we check applications immediately upon receipt or collect them all before checking. Finally, it appears that the applicant only has to submit an application to achieve employment. No interview required!

We could clarify all these issues with Robert and revise the model accordingly, but that's not the purpose of the strategic process model. Robert grasped the meaning of figure 3.4 with little explanation. It is doubtful that he would react well to our later diagrams if he encountered them when we weren't there to explain the symbols for the signal event or the different cardinalities of instances (one job posting, many applications). Robert wouldn't understand the model at first glance, and he wouldn't accept it any more. Consequently, we put figure 3.5 on the next page aside for further development at the operational level.

For strategic process models, we usually abstain from using multiple pools unless the customer is external to the organization. In such cases, a separate pool lets us model an

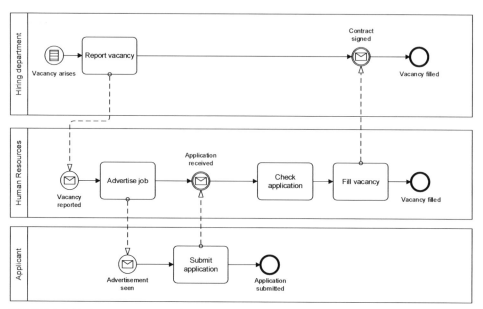

FIGURE 3.5 Each party is assigned its own pool.

overview of order processing, for instance, or complaint handling in the second pool. In figure 3.6, we show the customer as a collapsed pool so that we can focus on the process sequence at the time an order is received. Wouldn't it be nice if we could model all processes this way?

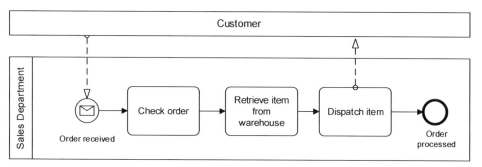

FIGURE 3.6 The customer as a collapsed pool.

We can't. The recruiting process example shows why we can't. In reality, we often have external partners that cannot be assigned to their own pools without making our strategic diagram so complex that it no longer serves our needs. On the other hand, we often deal with processes involving internal customers such as the hiring department in the recruiting process.

3.3.2   Tasks and subprocesses

Tasks often appear in our strategic models, but subprocesses appear only rarely. Task typing (see section 2.7.1 on page 54) is something we don't do for strategic process models though, and we also abstain from applying markers (see section 2.7.2 on page 56) with one exception: the loop marker. That is intuitive for most people, so we use it for strategic process models.

 Our BPMN Etiquette

When we explained tasks in section 2.2 on page 19, we said our convention is to use the *verb + object* pattern —"report vacancy," for example. When designating subprocesses at the strategic level, we do things a little differently. We nominalize them —turning "post job" into "job posting" and "check application" into "application checking." In some cases, nominalization produces something that sounds a little unfortunate, but there are two advantages: First, this practice differentiates tasks from subprocesses. Second, compared to tasks, subprocesses are discussed more often and in more depth. The nominalized forms help participants express themselves more constructively: "The application checking is still too complex. We have to...." Does this seem like splitting hairs? Is it pedantic? Our experience has shown that the devil is always in the details of project communication and software development. Careless language quickly leads to costly misconceptions; it is worth paying attention to such details.   ∎

Subprocesses should refine processes and process models. In the recruiting process model, we could define the steps "advertise job," "submit application," "check application," and "fill vacancy" as subprocesses. It's likely that they stand for complex operations and not simple tasks. From what Robert told us, the "report vacancy" task, however, seems to be limited to completing and sending an Excel spreadsheet. That doesn't sound like a complex operation, so we leave it as a task. To represent this thinking, we come up with figure 3.7 on the following page.

The question now is if we want to model collapsed subprocesses fully on the strategic level. Usually, we don't do that because the point of the strategic level is *not* to show detailed operational sequences. We can't make it correspond smoothly to the subprocesses level of detail anyway because of the semantic inconsistencies already described.

3.3.3   Gateways

The recruiting process shown in figure 3.7 on the next page is based on the assumption that we can fill vacancies when and as we like. That's not the reality, because sometimes we can't find a qualified candidate. We could model this and other special cases with gateways, but not at the strategic level.

At the strategic level, we only deal with the so-called "happy path," meaning that we show the process path and results that we'd *like* to see. Most of the time, the happy path is sufficient. But if a process has different triggers, as in a customer-driven process, for

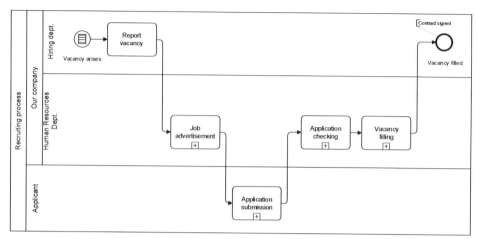

FIGURE 3.7 Differentiating tasks and subprocesses in the recruiting process.

example, we do sometimes have to model multiple paths at the strategic level. This is the time for a gateway.

We recommend using gateways as follows (refer to figure 3.8 on the facing page):

* Use XOR gateways for splits, that is, when *no* conditional flows exit directly from tasks. XOR gateways are easier to intuit than conditional flows. Target audiences understand a split when they see it.

* Merge tasks *without* XOR merge. In other words, let arrows flow directly into tasks. Such gateways (especially loops) only confuse inexperienced users; besides, omitting them results in more compact diagrams. Although we must use the gateways for merges in front of intermediate events and AND gateways, those should not appear at the strategic level.

* Use the AND gateway with *no* direct exit from the tasks to synchronize and make parallel. Parallel parts of a process need to be synchronized again later, so the AND gateway should be used in both cases to make the representation uniform and to avoid confusion.

* Do *not* use the OR gateway. It quickly results in meaningless constructs if you're not careful. Theoretically, you can represent any OR gateway by combining XOR and AND gateways. Again, however, this kind of complexity should not be part of a strategic diagram.

* Do *not* use the complex gateway. This representation of complex splitting and merging logics does not belong at the strategic level.

3.3.4 Events and event-based gateway

We recommend using start and end events at the strategic level to mark the start and the end of the process. You could do without these symbols, and the recruiting process would look like figure 3.9 on page 102. The diagram is more compact, but you can't see the

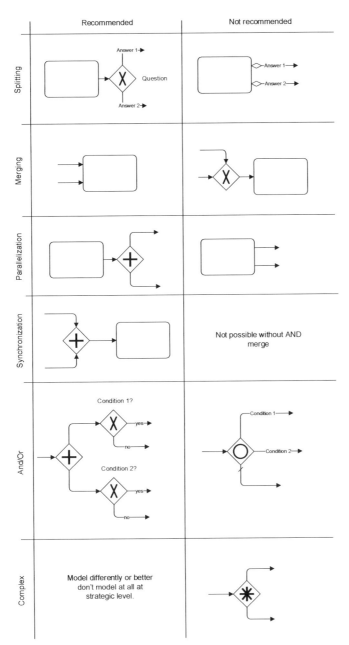

FIGURE 3.8 Recommended uses for gateways at the strategic level.

process trigger or its desired end condition. That's a particular problem for the start-to-end presentation we're trying to create at the strategic level.

Compared to start and end events, intermediate events often require a little explanation. It is difficult for many people to understand at the outset that a catching event means that

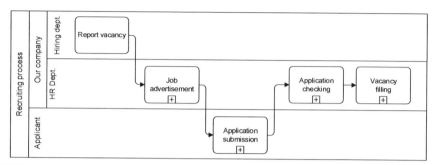

FIGURE 3.9 The recruiting process without start and end events.

the process waits for that event to occur. We have to label them descriptively to make the meaning clear. With the exception of none events, catching intermediate events are too complicated for the strategic level.

We only permit some of the possible event types at the strategic level:

None events may be used as start, intermediate, and end events. The intermediate event can indicate process status during the execution. Process owners readily accept this kind of status as milestones they can use to monitor progress. In figure 3.10, we show two milestones defined for the recruiting process. At the strategic level, process models are sometimes so clearly laid out that you could define a milestone for every step. In such lovely cases, it is probably better to leave explicit milestone indicators out of the diagram just for simplicity's sake.

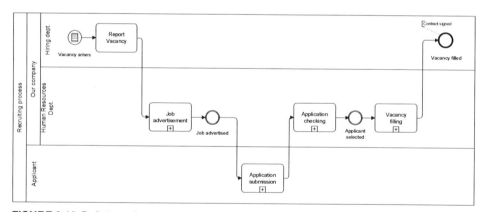

FIGURE 3.10 Defining milestones for the recruiting process.

We permit **message** and **timer** events as start events and intermediate events at the strategic level. The symbols are virtually self-explanatory.

The **conditional event** is problematic because people don't recognize it right away. It can be useful at the strategic level, however, because process owners want to see at a glance which conditions trigger a process or when a process has to execute. A common example is the tendering process, which, for compliance reasons, has to start as soon as an order exceeds a certain amount. This is why we include the conditional event in our strategic level "toolkit." We use it often.

We try to apply a type to every process start event. In other words, we model it as a message or a timer or a conditional event. We succeed almost every time. If none of these events apply, we consider first if we have chosen the correct process start —if our "pattern" matches the process, or if the process actually starts earlier or later than we thought. Once in a while, we model a none type start event at the strategic level. If we fully model a subprocess, that none start event is important for correct syntax because a subprocess can only be started by its parent process.

Intermediate events can be also attached to tasks and subprocesses, but we avoid using them in this context at the strategic level because they indicate an exception. We want to record only the standard sequence for now. We also exclude the event-based gateway from strategic diagrams; reacting to events is an inappropriate level of detail for the strategic level.

3.3.5   Data and artifacts

Text annotations are permitted at the strategic level. We use them often. In the recruiting process example, annotations helped us to add information to the "vacancy filled" end event, namely that the employment contract was signed at that point.

People easily understand the group frame, so it is permissible at the strategic level, but we find that it gets used infrequently because strategic models are clear enough without it. Inexperienced modelers often mistake the group frame for an expanded subprocess, so you may want to hide the group frame at first. You can reveal it after the modelers' understanding has grown.

Data objects quickly result in visual overload. On the other hand, they can make two things readily apparent:

1. The essential input and output parameters of a process or a subprocess.

2. The type of communications between process participants.

The second item technically is a message-flow domain. Because we deliberately avoid using multiple pools —and hence their message flows —at the strategic level, we resort to data objects.

When we ask the Human Resources manager, Robert, how information is transmitted in his recruiting process, he says, "We receive requirement notifications by email. We then post the job notices to our website and also on the major Internet job sites. We receive applications by postal mail and email, though the email responses have been growing as a proportion of the total."

We can model Robert's communication by using data objects attached to the sequence flows by means of associations (see figure 3.11 on the next page). We usually attach the essential input and output data to the sequence flow between the start event and the first task or between the last task and the end event. That may not be correct in a formal sense because the output is not passed to the end event, but it is intuitive and therefore workable at the strategic level.

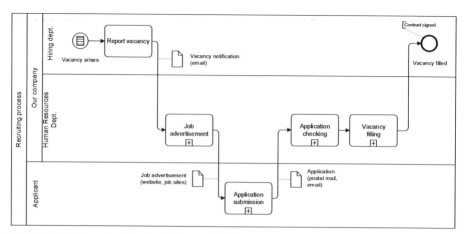

FIGURE 3.11 Data objects indicate forwarded information.

3.3.6   Custom artifacts

As described in Chapter 2, you can add your own symbols to BPMN as long as you only use them as artifacts. You can connect artifacts only by associations to flow objects (tasks, gateways, or events) to prevent them from influencing the sequence flow. They represent references to things beyond the main sequence.

In our experience, artifacts are well suited to the strategic level for meeting the particular requirements of your process owners. One classic is to represent the software systems used for individual tasks of subprocesses. We usually use a cuboid for this. The cuboid is used for the same purpose in Unified Modeling Language (UML) use case diagrams, which is why it makes sense to us.

When we ask what IT systems the recruiting process uses, Robert says, "So far almost none. The job description is created in Excel; all the other things are done without any special software." Find the corresponding representation in figure 3.12.

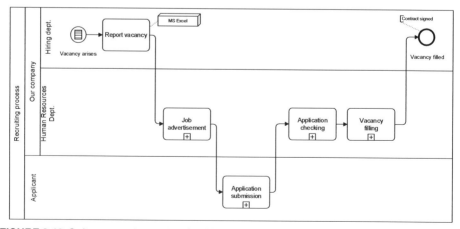

FIGURE 3.12 Software use is restricted to Microsoft Excel.

Depending on the industry and the particular needs, you can introduce custom artifacts for completely different purposes. Suppose the insurance sector faces regulatory pressure regarding minimum requirements for risk management. This makes identifying risks in the process documentation necessary; you can use a custom artifact to flag the risks associated with execution of tasks and subprocesses.

3.3.7 Hide and reveal symbols

You can see the extensions added to the recruiting example for milestones, data forwarding, and IT systems in figure 3.13. This information is particularly helpful for discussing a process, but because they tend to overload a diagram and add to the potential confusion, not all users of the diagram will want to see them. It is useful to be able to hide and reveal the extra symbols as needed. This is a question we often get in our BPMN workshops; here are our notes:

* Hiding and revealing is not a feature of the notation. This feature must be provided by the BPMN tool you work with.
* Several of the BPMN tools make it easy to hide and reveal artifacts such as data, annotations, or custom symbols.
* Hiding and revealing is more complicated for none intermediate events because they attach to the sequence flow. When you hide them, you get unexplained and unsightly gaps unless your tool is intelligent enough to rearrange the diagram accordingly. (Suppose an XOR merge was applied before an event that suddenly became redundant because the arrows could enter the task after the event directly.) So in general, hiding and revealing flow objects like activities, events, and gateways is problematic, which is why most BPMN tools do not provide a hide-reveal feature, or they limit its function.

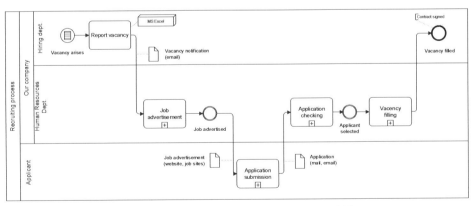

FIGURE 3.13 The recruiting process, including milestones, data, and IT systems.

■ 3.4   Process analysis on the strategic level

After making our first, rough survey of the recruiting process and documenting it, we can do two things:

1. We can start a detailed survey to model the actual state of the process at the operational level.

2. We can content ourselves with the documentation at the strategic level.

The choice depends on the purpose of the model. If we aim for ISO certification, or if we want to provide the model to process participants as a guide for their daily work, it needs to be more detailed.

Recall that our Human Resources manager is unhappy with his process, and he wants to embark on a project to improve it. He has described the symptomatic weaknesses. Remembering the BPM life cycle, we can now start with analysis to get to the bottom of the weaknesses and devise ideas for improvement (figure 3.14). A detailed survey and documentation of the current state can be helpful for this analysis, but to be honest, the cost-benefit ratio is high enough to discourage it in practice. More often than not, we use the strategic process model to guide our search for causes during analysis.

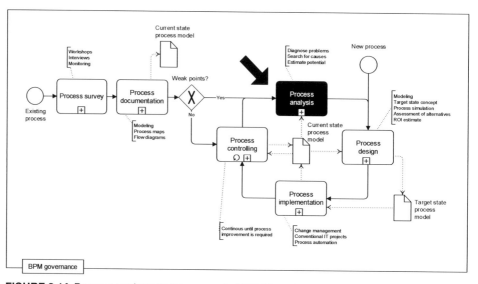

FIGURE 3.14 Process analysis in the camunda BPM life cycle.

How does searching for causes work? The main thing is that we listen. We listen not only to the process manager, but also to the customer of the process and, of course, to the process participants. How we proceed and what tools we use always depends on the complexity of the process, but a workshop or two involving these three parties is usually enough to identify the weak points of the process and their causes. We don't want to discuss the interpersonal and political aspects —these quickly become a problem in such workshops. Perhaps they are a topic for a different kind of book.

Here we draw a brief picture of a workshop called "Analysis of potentials in the recruiting process." The participants are:

- Process manager: Robert.
- Customer: Falko, Sales Manager and representative of the hiring departments.
- Process participants: Marina, Christine, and Stefan, clerks in the Human Resources Department.
- Process analyst: you!

After the usual introductions and explanations of purpose, you display the process model from figure 3.13 on page 105. You let it sink in. You apply your well-honed skills as a moderator to engage the participants in analyzing weak points. You list an obvious symptom, for instance, and ask the participants to confirm, correct, or amend your observation. You write the results on red index cards and attach them to a white board. They are:

- The process takes too long.
- The process is too intricate.
- The process is not transparent enough.

The complaint about the long processing time comes from Falko. Robert complains about the intricacy of the processing. Both of them agree that more transparency is needed to support comprehension of the process in whole and in its parts.

Working with the participants, you then extract the causes that account for the symptoms. Step by step, you identify and list on your red cards the causes of the causes. Some of the symptoms or causes may be attributable to a certain subprocess or task, and this will be well marked by the card affixed next to it. Other symptoms and causes will apply to the process as a whole.

All the workshop participants quickly agree that too many activities in the process are executed manually. "There must be a technical solution," is a unanimous verdict.

Robert's criticism that the vacancy notifications from the hiring departments are often incomplete, unclear, or incorrect, is of course not received enthusiastically by Falko, but Falko cannot deny that mere notification is usually insufficient. More clarifying details have to change hands between the hiring departments and HR.

For his part, Falko faults the Excel template provided by HR for the notifications. "These things are a catastrophe! Confusing and without any assistance or explanation. You can't even see which details are mandatory and which are optional!"

One ticklish issue involves holding times: the periods between task assignments and when they actually occur. Robert and Falko blame each other. They accuse and defend their respective staffs without useful facts to back up their statements. At this juncture, you, as diplomatic moderator, get the squabblers to agree that excess holding times harm the process, but that the causes cannot yet be clearly established nor responsibility apportioned.

The result of the workshop is the causal chain as shown in figure 3.15 on the following page. You deduce four solutions to be pursued within the scope of an improvement project:

- Reduce manual activities.
- Minimize correction loops.
- Make the current status of each operation visible at all times.

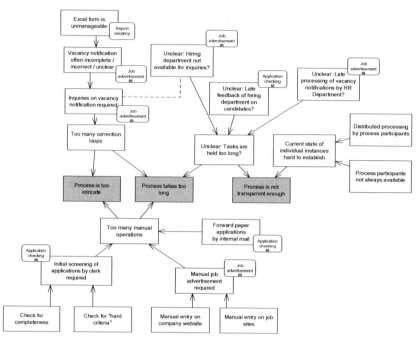

FIGURE 3.15 Causal chain, showing weaknesses and their causes.

- Record and assign responsibility for idle times.

You may suppose that the solutions will be IT-enabled, though that's not always the case in practice. We do not mean to suggest that software is the solution to every problem. BPMN development started with the need to improve processes by means of IT, however, and that is why our example reflects that kind of scenario.

In the BPM life cycle, you now enter the "process design" phase to devise an improved target-state process. This is the time for the operational level.

3.5   Conversations and choreographies

The possibilities provided by BPMN 2.0 for modeling conversations and choreographies haven't yet established themselves in real-world situations. We don't find them in our customers' projects, and we only use them on rare occasions. If you're interested, the next section provides some thoughts about using them in the described use case.

Looking at the recruiting process as a conversation (figure 3.16 on the next page), two possibilities present themselves: In the simplest case, just represent that there are three participants in the process and that they are conversing with each other. The other possibility is to add a multiple symbol to the applicant to show that, while only one hiring department and the Human Resources Department participate in the conversation, more than one applicant may participate. Certainly it helps to indicate the different cardinalities, but the success of doing so depends on users who understand the symbols. Apart from that, the conversation diagram is good for representing all the parties in a single view.

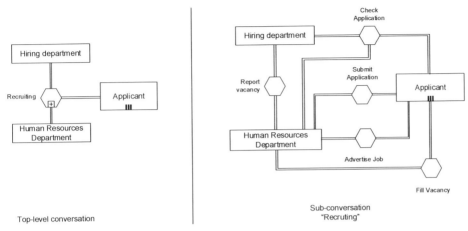

Top-level conversation

Sub-conversation
"Recruting"

FIGURE 3.16 The recruiting process conversation at two levels of granularity.

We can refine this conversation and fully model its sub-conversations. The plus sign in the hexagon of the top-level representation indicates a refinement similar to the symbol for a subprocess in our process diagrams. We can see in the refined representation that not all the participants participate in all sub-conversations. The applicants, for example, do not participate in the vacancy notifications; the hiring department doesn't participate in posting the job.

There's a semantic problem with this representation: The job posting is not a message received directly by the applicant; it is modeled by means of the conversational relationship. We tend to allow the semantic flaw in the interests of clearness and comprehensibility, just as in our process diagrams. One advantage a conversation diagram has over the sequential representation in a process diagram is that we can take the different communications relationships between participants into account without having to accept a complicated representation with multiple pools and their related message flows.

The representation as a choreography in figure 3.17 on the following page is even more precise because it also considers the order of communication. We can see the different messages. It is a mixture of conversation and process diagrams because we still see the various participants in the choreography of tasks and subprocesses. One advantage in this is the more differentiated examination of cardinalities: The job advertisement takes place once, and it is a message from the Human Resources Department to a number of applicants. (No, the semantics are not really correct, but we accept this for simplicity's sake.)

In the next, "application submission" step, multiple applicants send their applications to the Human Resources Department. It is correct to represent "application submission" without a multiple instance, because this subprocess is executed only once by each applicant. The application check, conversely, is executed as often as applications are

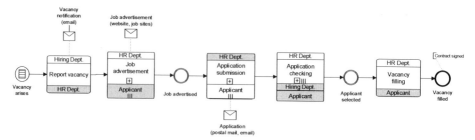

FIGURE 3.17 The recruiting process as a choreography.

received, in other words, multiple times. It is completed separately for each applicant, however, which has its effect on the "applicant" communication partner. Each applicant gets a separate invitation and a separate interview, so the applicant gets no multiple instance symbol in this subprocess. The last subprocess, "vacancy filling," takes place only once, and the chosen applicant signs a contract.

The advantage of the choreography diagram is that it compactly represents the communications relationship between process participants. It is ideal for providing overviews of communication-intensive processes. The question is if choreography diagrams can be understood and accepted by target groups at the strategic level. In our experience, it is hard enough to introduce the regular symbols of BPMN to such groups.

4 Operational process models

■ 4.1 About this chapter

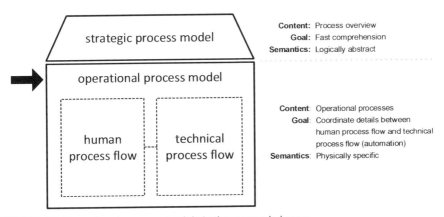

FIGURE 4.1 Operational process models in the camunda house

4.1.1 Purpose and benefit

It is at the operational level that process models begin to reveal operational details in the form of human and technical flows. Process participants reference operational process models (the human flows, that is) every day. Process analysts examine them to identify improvements. Also, operational process diagrams can be the starting point for technical process implementation in the form of technical flows —ideally by a process engine. The operational process model obviously describes more detail than does the strategic model, but this leads to a problem:

A whole process is a complex interaction between people and IT systems as they carry out tasks. The **process analyst** is concerned with getting to the heart of these interactions so that he or she can devise organizational or technical improvements. The analyst's question is:

How is the work done, and how can we do it better?

The **process participant** only cares about the aspects of the process that concern him directly. He wants to know:

How should I do my work?

When a process requires technology to be implemented, the **process engineer** gets involved. He or she has to understand what the technical implementation is meant to achieve from a functional point of view. The process engineer asks him- or herself:

What does the engine have to achieve?

It isn't easy to reconcile the three roles, and answering their questions is the challenge of the operational level. If you meet the challenge successfully, the benefits are:

- The logic of the operational process model is consistent between operations and the technical implementation. In other words, the process actually works as documented.
- The understanding gap between business and IT shrinks. The parties can discuss the same process model, and they can recognize both the technical effects of business requirements and the impact technical implementations may have on operations.
- If the process is implemented by a process engine, monitoring and reporting on the process can become much more substantial and immediate.

In short, if you master the operational level, you will have found the common language of business and IT —at least as far as process modeling is concerned.

4.1.2 Model requirements

Just as with the strategic level, operational process diagrams must be syntactically correct. Although some semantic irregularities can be tolerated at the strategic level, we can't allow them in operational models. The operational level describes how work is actually done, so there can be neither contradictions in content nor formal mistakes.

As you develop the operational model for any project that includes technical implementation by means of a process engine, another requirement arises: All the questions that the process engineer must ask to understand the desired outcomes need to be answered. After all, the technical model itself becomes executable.

Precision serves the process participants too, because they should be able to refer to the model for how to accomplish the work. At the same time, it is best not to burden participants with complexity that doesn't serve them. After all, the participants' core competence is the work itself, not BPM. For participants, the process model is just a means to an end, something they may reference only once in a while.

4.1.3 Procedure

An operational process model has to be sufficiently precise but not overly complicated. To achieve that apparently contradictory goal, we provide a view of the process model specific to each role. Figure 4.2 on the next page depicts what we mean. If the process participants see a view that represents only their perspective, they are satisfied. The participants know what to do and when to wait for others to complete their portions of the process without being distracted by the details of what the others do.

Viewer	Process **participant**	Process **analyst**	Process **engineer**
Central problem	How should I do my work?	How is the work done?	What does the engine do?
View	Own orchestration	Entire collaboration	Orchestration of the process engine

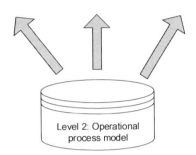

Level 2: Operational process model

FIGURE 4.2 The roles and their views at the operational level.

The core idea of the operational level is to differentiate consistently between orchestration and collaboration. As explained in section 2.9 on page 71, each participant gets his or her own pool. This presents the participant's experience as its own, closed process. Reserve the diagram that shows the collaboration among these processes for the process analyst, who presumably can handle the complexity.

Treat the process engine as a participant with its own pool, and the process engineer can focus on it. Note that in this approach we are following the BPMN idea of a conductor for each pool who controls its processes. BPMN presumes a process engine even when a human serves in place of an actual process engine.

Aside from the improved views, this differentiation is important because in practice, the entire process is almost never controlled completely by a process engine. There are always decisions to be made and tasks to be carried out by humans. To represent the process completely in a model, we have to account for the human activities. We accomplish this when we assign a separate pool to each participant, whether human or not.

The process analyst plays a major role in achieving a differentiated model. He or she must comprehend BPMN fully and be able to model the process from different participants' points of view. If the target state process is to be implemented in a process engine, he or she must develop and maintain the model in all its representations, from the strategic to the technical.

This is an example of the process analyst's steps:

1. Review the target state process at the strategic level. (See chapter 3.)
2. Resolve the lanes into separate pools. (See section 4.2 on the next page.)
3. Model the human flows, that is, the target-state process from each participant's point of view. (The participants and the process manager must settle upon these details. See section 4.3 on page 116.)

4. Model what the participants do that will be supported by the process engine and how it will do so. This also must be settled between the manager and participants. (See section 4.4 on page 119.)

5. Model the technical flows, at least to the extent that these can be derived from the participants' processes. The process analyst or the process engineer can do this. The operational model won't be directly executable, but the process engineer can enhance the model for that purpose. (See section 4.4.2 on page 122.)

6. Finalize and document other requirements such as templates, data, and business rules. Group these around the process model by referencing them from their relevant symbols in the diagram (See section 4.4.3 on page 123.)

This is only one approach. If it makes sense to you, you can start from the technical flow and work "bottom up," or you can work outward from an operational process model. Frequently, it is the operational process model that comes into existence first because the business and IT got together during a workshop, and they developed the human and technical flows concurrently.

After developing the model, show the views to the people affected. This takes a tool with good presentation functions. The ability to expand and collapse pools is especially valuable, since the expand/collapse function means you can avoid having a lot of different diagrams with redundantly modeled pools. For more on tool support for BPMN in general and our framework in particular, see section 6.4.2 on page 196.

■ 4.2 From the strategic level to the operational level

We often create a strategic model of the process before we model it at the operational level. For our recruiting process example, we created the strategic process model in section 3.2 on page 95. We depicted it in figure 4.3 on the facing page, and in section 3.4 on page 106, we discussed the process' weak points. We learned that the process sequence itself is not that bad; most of the friction comes from insufficient technological support. Now the process modeling needs to extend to the operational level. First, we'll examine the sequence solely from an organizational standpoint. Second, we'll think through what a process engine can contribute to improving the process.

Chapter 3 described how strategic process models often contain semantic contradictions. These make it impossible to refine the model directly, but strategic views often differ significantly from operational views. You can assume that a strategic process model rarely changes. At the operational level, you can expect changes more often. That's another reason for the principal structure of models at this level to be technically compatible with the even more detailed implementation models to follow.

As a consequence, while we will reference the strategic process model often, we have to develop the operational model afresh. That may sound like a problem, but in practice it usually is not: The strategic model doesn't take that much time to create, and it achieves clarity about strategic purposes and outcomes that you shouldn't need to revisit while

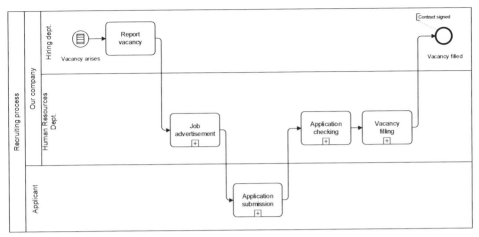

FIGURE 4.3 The recruiting process at the strategic level.

developing at the operational model. Also, because the strategic level changes so infrequently, you need not worry about duplicating effort to maintain it through updates.

The recruiting process example has a semantic difficulty at the strategic level: the different cardinality of instances. It looks as though every applicant for a job gets that job, even though everyone understands that's not the real-world expectation. Everyone assumes that the normal course of events is that several applicants submit applications, that Human Resources checks a corresponding number of applications, and that a single applicant ultimately fills the vacancy. Another difficulty is that we don't know our applicants nor their number. These are two reasons that, when it comes to creating an operational model, we cannot represent the applicant as a lane in the same pool as the other participants.

A valid operational model also has to specify the interaction between the hiring department and Human Resources more realistically. It's not as if HR carries out the "job advertisement" and "application checking" tasks without consulting the hiring department. The process analysis (section 3.4 on page 106) showed that the two departments communicate actively; it is the ineffectiveness of their communication that causes most of the friction and ambiguity. What makes the most sense therefore is to model the processes of these participants in separate pools. That allows an explicit examination of the organizational interfaces. It also allows us to provide each participant with information relevant to his or her role, and we can exclude irrelevant information. Irrelevant information is a huge over-complication!

Figure 4.4 on the next page shows the recruiting process after moving the lanes into separate pools and accounting for the activities that require exchanges between participants. The applicant still reacts to the signal of a job being advertised, but the three short lines at the bottom center of the applicant pool indicate that there potentially are multiple applicants. (Refer to section 2.9.5 on page 77.) The possibility of multiple applicants is why we modeled an AND split after the message "application received" event; it shows that HR is not waiting for a single application but will instead process any

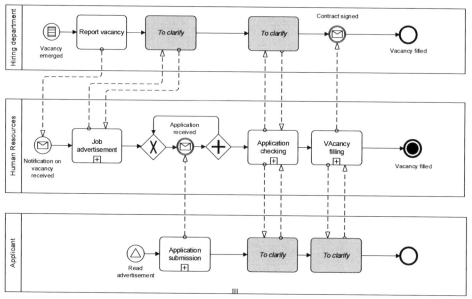

FIGURE 4.4 Start of transfer to the operational level.

applications received. The terminate event at the end of the HR pool means that this activity will continue only until an applicant is selected and successfully employed.

Open issues remain to be settled and modeled. Not only do we have to define the "to be clarified" activities, but we have possible special cases to account for. What if:

- an applicant is rejected as unqualified?
- not even one applicant is qualified?
- not even one application is received?

Examining this entire process at the operational level easily could exceed this book's goal of illustrating principles and methods. In the following sections, therefore, we elaborate only on the part starting with identifying the personnel requirement through advertising the job. (To explore the complete example, visit BPM-Guide.de/BPMN.)

■ 4.3   Processes of the participants

As already described, the process analyst models processes at the operational level. Where does he or she get the operational details needed? Usually from the process participants themselves, that is, the people working in the process. For the "post a job" process, we'll interview Falko first, because he's the manager of the hiring department. Falko describes his contribution this way:

"When I see that we need a new staff member, I report the vacancy to Human Resources. I then wait for them to send me the job description so that I can check it before they publish the advertisement. I may have to request a correction to the job description, but otherwise I release it. And sometimes HR has additional questions about tasks or qualifications, so I make myself available for clarifications."

When we model Falko's process, we may include the Human Resources clerk in the diagram to complete the picture. When we collapse the clerk's pool, however, figure 4.5 results.

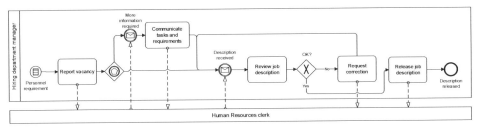

FIGURE 4.5 The "post a job" process from the hiring department manager's point of view.

Note: BPMN 2.0 does not allow sequence flows to flow directly into an intermediate event following an event gateway. This prohibition seems unnecessary to us, and we advocate that it be removed in future versions of the specification. For the time being, try representing this type of scenario as shown in figure 4.6.

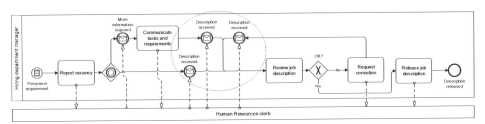

FIGURE 4.6 The current version of BPMN 2.0 requires this representation, which seems inefficient and unnecessary.

Christine, the Human Resources clerk, has a different point of view about the "post a job" process: "When a job vacancy is reported to me, I write a job description based on the details I'm given," she says. "If there are ambiguities in those details, I have to ask the hiring department about them. After I finish the description, I submit it to the hiring department for it to be checked, then I wait for it to be released. Sometimes they do that right away, but sometimes they reject it and ask for corrections. In that case, I correct the description and submit it again to be checked. Once the description is finally released, I publish the advertisement for the job."

When we collapse Falko's pool and show Christine's, the result looks like figure 4.7 on the next page.

What have we achieved so far? We have explicitly modeled the operational details of the "post a job" process. At the same time, we created two process models that are not overly complicated on their own.

The consumers of our models must have some basic knowledge of BPMN. They must:

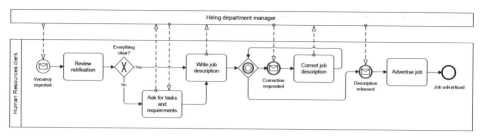

FIGURE 4.7 The "post a job" process from the Human Resources clerk's point of view.

* understand events —intermediate events in particular.
* understand the difference between a data-based and an event-based gateway.
* understand the difference between the sequence and the message flow.

The burden on the users of our models is greater at the operational level than it is at the strategic level. The first target audience for the operational level is the process analyst, who can use the model as the basis for a detailed analysis as well as for an IT implementation. We show this later. In all likelihood, the process analyst developed the model in BPMN, so his or her understanding of the model can be presumed.

The second target audience is the participants whose work the model represents —Falko and Christine. They should be partners with the process analyst in a dialog about improvements, and they should at least understand the models. You may find them both later using the diagrams as a guideline for their work, helping to answer the questions "How should I do my work?" and "What do I have to do next?"

So, will participants like Christine and Falko accept the models? Our experience shows that they will, provided that:

* Each participant sees only his or her own pool and not the full complexity of the process. This requires that the process model be developed accordingly and an adequate tool used to present it.
* The participants were provided with a basic briefing on BPMN, and a simple key or legend to explain the symbols. As the process analyst, you probably will have to do the instruction yourself. Tools often provide a key or legend.

Of course we can view "post a job" as a whole by expanding both pools, and we can show it to Christine and Falko as a detailed collaboration diagram (figure 4.8 on the facing page). But isn't it obvious how much more complicated this diagram is, compared to separate views of the pools? Would the process participants be more likely or less likely to accept and use the more complex diagram? In any event, the entire collaboration only matters to the process analyst. In the following two sections, we will deal with collaboration diagrams as we consider process automation.

BPMN 2.0 provides the option to hide the complexities of the collaboration in a choreography diagram (figure 4.9 on the next page). The advantage is that this represents the interaction between participants more compactly. It is therefore good for orienting the process analyst. On the other hand, a choreography diagram omits internal steps that do not help communication between participants. You can't see, for example, that the Human Resources clerk executes the "advertise job" task. We regard choreography

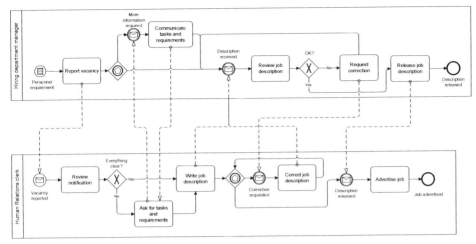

FIGURE 4.8 "Post a job" as a collaboration diagram.

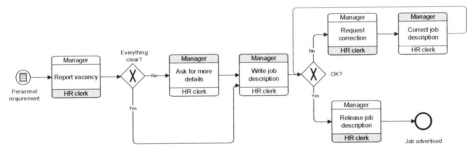

FIGURE 4.9 "Post a job" as a choreography diagram.

diagrams as sometimes useful additions to operational level collaboration diagrams, but usually they can't take the place of collaborations.

▪ 4.4 Preparing for process automation

Describing a process from an organizational perspective is only one task of modeling a process at the operational level. It's not even the most interesting task! The holy grail actually is the smooth transfer from human to technical flows, in other words, from the functional to the executable process model.

In section 1.1.4 on page 5, we show how an executable process model can be interpreted directly by a process engine to combine human workflow with service orchestration. Since this is also central to the IT perspective on BPM, we focus on this approach in the following sections and in Chapter 5 (see figure 4.10 on the next page). An alternative would be to implement the process logic without a process engine, but in a general

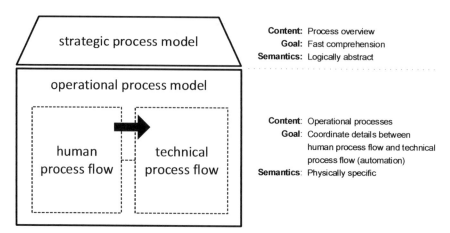

FIGURE 4.10 We focus on the transfer from human to technical flows.

programming language such as Java or C#. That's a scenario we'll address in section 4.4.5 on page 126.

4.4.1   Designing for support by a process engine

The desired technical implementation for a process can be discussed and documented with the models we did for the individual participants. Let's now consider the participants as users of software, and let's see what performance they expect from an automated process. In this thought experiment, the process engine itself becomes a participant with which the user exchanges messages.

Falko, as hiring department manager, describes the desired support in the "post a job" process:

"I record a vacancy in a form on our portal and then send it. If the job description is ready to be checked, I want to see it in my to-do list on the portal. I process the task by reading the description, and I either request corrections or I release it. After the job advertisement runs, I want a short email notice that everything worked out."

If you remember Falko's process model from figure 4.5 on page 117, you will recognize his description, but there are two major differences:

* The Human Resources Department's reaction to requests is not to be shown as a task on the portal. It is still processed by email or phone.

* The confirmation message about successful postings is new.

Now we expand on the process model:

* We subdivide it into lanes called "HR portal" and "Other."

* We assign all the tasks to be executed on the portal to its lane. For our purposes, a message event represents a human task that displays in the task list. A task with an outgoing message flow means that the user has completed a human task. The XOR gateway shows that the task may have different results, such as "request correction" or "release job description."

- The first task in the HR portal lane is "report vacancy." This is not a task that was assigned to the user by the process engine because it does not follow the corresponding message event. It is possible, however, for the user to trigger the process, that is, to effect an instantiation. If so, the process engine must provide the corresponding option, usually by means of a form available on the portal, which can be filled in at any time.
- The request made by the Human Resources Department, as well as the reaction to it, are assigned to the Other lane because neither are realized on the portal, but rather through the usual channels: phone or email. The message conveying that the advertisement was published also belongs in the Other lane. Although the process engine sends that message, it reaches the user by email, and not as a notification in the portal.

The result is in figure 4.11, which shows the process engine as another participant, but still with the pool collapsed.

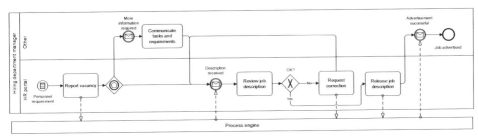

FIGURE 4.11 IT support of the hiring department's manager regarding the job posting.

Now we learn something new from Christine, the Human Resources clerk: "A vacancy report appears as a new entry in the task list of the HR portal. This is where I write the job description and then forward it to the hiring department for verification. Forwarding it completes the task. If I have to correct the description, that comes up on my task list too. If the hiring department releases the job description, however, I essentially receive notice by the appearance of an "initiate advertisement" task. In that case, I specify the advertising channels on the portal and then initiate the advertisement. If the advertisement runs successfully, I want a short notice that everything worked out."

Applying the principles discussed in this chapter results in figure 4.12, but with one difference: The user doesn't trigger the process any more. Falko already took care of this. Christine only has to react to the new entry in her task list on the portal. You will recognize this by the start event of the message type.

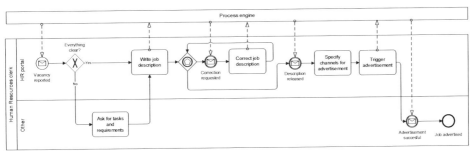

FIGURE 4.12 IT support of the Human Resources clerk.

4.4.2   Required processes of the process engine

We will now define the first version of the technical flow. As process analysts, we don't need as much input from the process participants now. We can turn our attention to the process engineer. We consult with the process engineer to determine how to implement the process with the process engine. We show the pools of the human participants in a collaboration diagram, and we expand the pool of the process engine as another participant, dividing the process engine pool into three lanes:

- The hiring department manager gets a lane, as does the Human Resources clerk. All the tasks placed in these lanes are user tasks, which is to say, tasks for humans to complete.
- The third lane is for fully automated tasks. These are things like interface calls (service tasks) or internal program fragments (script tasks). You can also store whole subprocesses in this lane.

The process steps to be implemented in the engine result directly from the behavior of users Falko and Christine. The process starts because Falko reports a vacancy by filling in a form on the portal. He sends it, which is represented by the start event of the message type. The process engine then assigns the "write job description" task to Christine. Once Christine completes her task, the engine assigns the "check job description" task to Falko. Falko can either release the description or ask for a correction. Depending on Falko's choice, the engine will assign either "trigger advertisement" or "correct job description" to Christine. If she has to correct it, the job description returns to Falko as another "check job description" task. This loop repeats until Falko releases the job description.

The engine assigns "trigger advertisement" to Christine after Falko releases the description. First, she has to specify the channels through which the job is to be advertised, and then she has to initiate the action. This tells the engine that Christine has completed "trigger advertisement." The engine then executes the "publish advertisement" subprocess, which consists mainly of interface calls. (It is encapsulated as a subprocess at this point in order to avoid overloading the diagram.) At the end, the process engine sends confirmation emails to both Falko and Christine to inform them that the advertisement was successfully published.

The collaboration diagram in figure 4.13 on the facing page shows the technical process flow, which is executable in the process engine. There is some redundancy within the diagram because the users are represented in their own pools, but they also have lanes in the pool for the process engine. This is important for separating responsibilities: The participants always decide on the routing within a pool, that is, they determine which path exits an XOR gateway.

Christine, for example, decides if she can write the job description without further input or if she has to get Falko to clear up discrepancies. The process engine can't do that; it doesn't even notice this decision. On the other hand, the process engine does decide if Christine needs to execute "correct job description" or "trigger advertisement" next because the corresponding XOR gateway is in its pool. The process engine makes this decision based on Falko's decision following his review.

Our collaboration diagram solves a problem that arises frequently when attempting to evolve a functional (operational) process model into an executable one: mixing control instances in a single pool. As we keep saying, people and process engines almost always

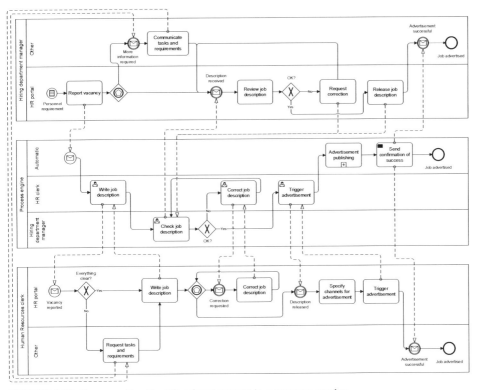

FIGURE 4.13 Representing the job advertisement in a process engine.

have their respective decisions to make within a process. Until you segregate control instances into appropriate pools, it will be difficult to achieve a model that you can execute in a process engine.

Another advantage to this approach is that we still can present views optimized for our targeted groups of users:

* The process analyst can see the entire collaboration diagram.
* The process engineer can see only the process engine's pool.
* The process participants can see their own pools only. Not only are these pools less complex than the whole collaboration diagram, but they also contain additional information not part of the process engine's pool: that inquiries are made in case of discrepancies, for instance.

Our judgment is that this approach is the only practical way to align business and IT in a BPMN process model.

4.4.3   Further requirements

Could our process engineer implement the process from the diagram as shown? Probably, but there are issues still to be settled, such as the templates to be displayed and the exact tasks in a vacancy notification or a job description. These are typical kinds of requirements for any software project, however, and they do not affect the process logic. We don't recommend documenting these requirements directly in BPMN; instead, we suggest linking them to the process at appropriate points. That way, the process represents a central starting point for requirements documentation. Of course, your BPMN tool must support linking.

We have categorized typical requirements as they occur in projects for the development of process applications in figure 4.14. Besides BPMN, we use graphic screen designs, class diagrams, decision tables, and text to document requirements. In integration-intensive projects, we use, among other tools, diagrams to describe system landscapes.

Type	Explanation	Examples	Notations	BPD link
Functional	Functions to be provided by the solution	- Process logic - Features - Use cases - Interfaces - Business logic	- BPMN - UML (use cases) - User stories - Acceptance tests - General text	- Task
Non-functional	Properties to be met by the software	- Service level Agreements (SLA) - Response time - Capacity - Maintainability - Platform compatibility	- Text	- Pool
User interface	Channels through which the user interacts with the software	- Masks - Dialog work flows - Mobile devices - E-mail roles	- BPMN - Mask sketches - User stories - Acceptance tests	- Task
Data	Data to be processed by the software	- Contents - Restrictions - Formats - Channels - Mappings	- ER diagrams - UML (class diagrams) - Spreadsheets	- Pool - Data objects
Rules	Specifications according to which the software is to decide	- Validations - Checks - Calculations - Control points	- Spreadsheets - Trees - Text	- Task

FIGURE 4.14 Typical requirements for implementing an executable process.

You can see drafts of screens and confirmation emails for the job advertisement process and how they link to the process model in figure 4.15 on the facing page. Sometimes you can derive the control elements to be provided on the screens from participants' pools. We know, for example, that Falko can release a job description or request a correction. That may imply the need for option buttons (also known as radio buttons) on the form Falko sees. Options representing advertising channels may be needed for Christine.

4.4.4   Technical implementation beyond the process engine

In your BPM projects, you often will find that you have to implement certain software components beyond the process engine. For us, this happens most often with:

- Business logic and rules
- Screens and screen flows
- Data transformations

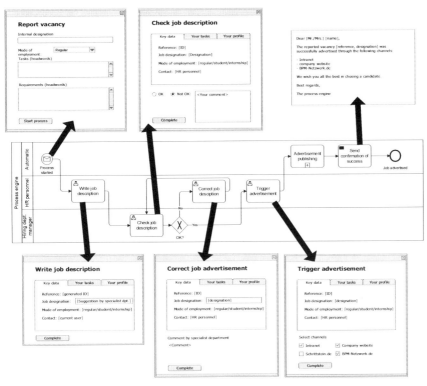

FIGURE 4.15 Drafts of screens and email for job advertisement.

4.4.4.1 Business logic and rules

Business logic is, for example, a calculation to be programmed. It is appropriate to package the calculations as services so that the process engine can call them through service tasks. This builds direct reference to the paradigm of service-oriented architecture (SOA). Business rules can be represented in a rule engine, and they can be called from the process engine through custom-developed, business-rule tasks as of BPMN 2.0. We deal with this subject in section 4.5.4 on page 135 and section 5.8 on page 176.

In either case, it usually makes sense not to model the respective requirements fully in BPMN. A better solution is simply to reference business logic or rules in the process diagram through service or business rule tasks.

4.4.4.2 Screen flows

Screen flows are a borderline case because, from the process automation perspective, they serve only to execute a single task. It also is difficult to do if the sequence of screens varies with the entries a user makes or with the data established between screens. Screen flows, however, are also processes. UML activity diagrams have been used often to model them, which suggests that BPMN can as well.

Clean BPM architecture strictly separates screen flows from the process model. In other words, a process engine is only loosely coupled to a screen flow application by means of clearly defined interfaces. To be consistent about this, you have to define a separate pool for the screen flow application and link it to the process engine and to the user with message flows. From the application's perspective, each screen flow is an isolated process. If your process contains several screen flows, you must create a separate pool for each one, even though the same screen flow application controls them all.

If that seems too complicated, or if your process engine combines the screen flow control with the executable process model, you can set it aside and model the screen flow as a collaboration between user and process engine. We can't recommend doing so, however, because it leads to process models that are less serviceable and more error-prone. It may be a good compromise to package screen flows in an embedded subprocess.

4.4.4.3   Data transformations

Data transformations are required primarily in integration-intensive processes. A clean BPM architecture requires that the process model be decoupled from the details of the interface calls. At this point, the Enterprise Service Bus (ESB) comes in, and you should represent it as a separate pool and handle it as you would a screen-flow application. You can likewise integrate these steps directly in the process model of the process engine by working with script tasks.

Script tasks represent internal steps of the process engine. Data transformations are an example. You could wrap the data transformation in a service and call it through a service task. The difference is that the transformation engine (an XSLT processor that transforms XML data, for instance) would be a component internal to the process engine if it were a script task. It would be provided by an external component —that is, from the perspective of the process engine —if it were a service task.

4.4.5   Technical implementation without process engine

Perhaps you don't use a process engine to execute the technical process flows. Perhaps you program it in Java, C#, or another classic programming language. This doesn't matter for the transition from the strategic level to the operational; your compiler or interpreter equates to the process engine. Doing without a process engine may mean that you cannot execute the process logic directly from an operational process model. Another specification —called requirements specification, or detailed technical specification —will be required instead before the implementation. The process diagrams developed at the operational level can be integrated in this IT specification to form the basis of the technical design.

In conventional software development, requirements are often established without an end-to-end perspective of a process. Instead, they provide a compilation of functions that a user executes in a specified order, depending on the process to be carried out. These functions can be defined as applications or "use cases" in the design phase, which brings us to the classic domain of the Unified Modeling Language (UML).

You can apply BPM and our framework to such projects, but remember that each use case represents an independent process. You have to define a separate pool for each use case.

Compared to implementing in a process engine, the user has responsibility for linking the use cases into a process that could be represented in a single pool.

Occasionally, the same use case can apply to different scenarios. We recommend modeling the respective roles as simple processes that package the use cases as subprocesses. Figure 4.16 shows two examples of that procedure. Between the pools, you see a UML use case diagram that joins the use cases. This is an example that shows UML and BPMN working well together. Figure 4.17 on the following page shows the fully modeled "login" use case.

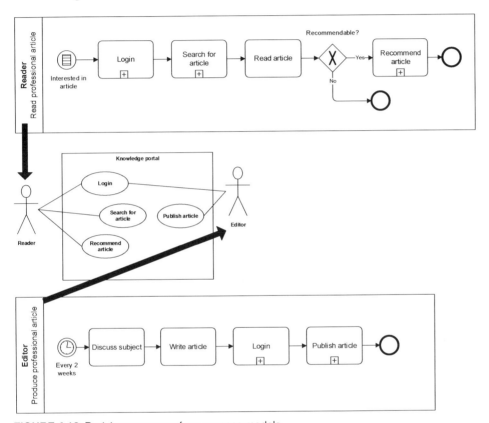

FIGURE 4.16 Deriving use cases from process models.

We can state as a principle that BPMN can benefit conventional IT projects compared to other process notations. As we pointed out earlier, however, BPMN was not developed for that purpose but rather to support projects with a process engine in mind. Perhaps the more important point is that it makes little sense to do process-intensive IT projects without a process engine.

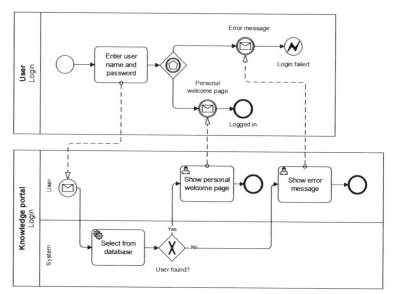

FIGURE 4.17 The "login" use case as a fully modeled collaboration of user and software.

■ 4.5   Hands-on tips for the operational level

4.5.1   From the happy path to the bitter truth

4.5.1.1   The First Pass Yield and BPMN

The field of organizational process management defines First Pass Yield (FPY) as the "percentage of units that meet specifications in the first process run without need of rework or repair."

You can well imagine that a major goal of process optimization involves maximizing FPY. Traditional organizational process consultants have applied various analytical methods successfully for years, but these methods are based on key figures such as error rates or processing times. Such measures have to be either estimated or manually established in organizational process management, methods that are laborious and error-prone.

Wouldn't it be exciting to integrate the FPY concept into the world of modern BPM (and BPMN)? After all, key figures can be measured with comparative ease, precisely, and in real time by a process engine.

To accomplish this integration, first understand how the FPY approach works in traditional sequence notations. Look at the sequence plan process model in figure 4.18 on the next page, which is suitable for FPY analysis, and which we compare to BPMN in section 2.12.3 on page 84).

Notice that there is a "main path" running from the top left straight down to the result. Anything that needs a change follows the "correction path." We can assume that the main path is the path that the process manager desires; it is also referred to as the "happy path." The probability that a result is not okay and needs correction is 30% in this model. Conversely, 70% of the results do not need correction —that's the FPY. We can analyze key

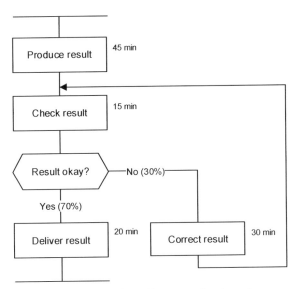

FIGURE 4.18 A process as a sequence plan with a correction branch.

figures recorded with the tasks, such as processing time, by various analytical methods to assess Key Performance Indicators (KPI). In this simple example, we could state three things about the running time of the process:

Variant	Time
First Pass Yield	80 minutes
Worst Case	110 minutes
Average	89 minutes

The average here results from the calculation: (FPY * 0.7) + (worst case * 0.3) = 56 + 33 = 89 minutes. This is also called "variational calculation," for which a non-iterative procedure is applied for simplicity. The assumption is that the result must be corrected only once, if at all, per instance. (If you want to learn more about these methods and you read German, we recommend the work by Guido Fischermanns.)

Could we apply the FPY approach in BPMN? Generally, yes. We showed in section 2.12.4 on page 84 how to store calculated key figures and average running times in process diagrams. Our "job advertisement" case has two possible correction loops:

1. When the vacancy report is not sufficient for Christine's purposes, she has to ask Falko for clarification. We assume in the process model that this is required only once.

2. When Falko does not like the job description, he asks Christine to correct it. According to the process model, this loop could repeat infinitely. We would apply a non-iterative method to assess the key figures.

We modeled the job-advertising process at the operational level from three perspectives, so we should apply the FPY methodology to three different pools for Falko, Christine, and the process engine. If we show the process from end to end in the process engine, it will be enough to examine its pool to apply the FPY approach.

The collaboration diagram (figure 4.13 on page 123) shows clearly which parts of the process are directly captured by the process engine's measurements and which are not. We derive this knowledge from the process modeled in its pool:

1. The process engine can measure the running time of these tasks: "write job description," "check job description," "correct job description," and "trigger advertisement"; and of the "advertisement publishing" subprocess.

2. It can also measure the number of times the job description needs to be corrected.

You can analyze these key figures with an appropriate reporting engine. (Or, when in doubt, just use Microsoft Excel for a defined number of process instances, average them, and create colorful diagrams to make your top managers happy.) But we also see which steps the process engine cannot measure. It doesn't see the times that Christine has to repeat her request for clarification to Falko. It therefore can't record the rate of occurrence for these necessary correction loops nor can it store that information for analysis. It also does not know how long a clarification takes. From the engine's point of view, all this is part of the "write job description" task, which it assigned to Christine. This may lead to distorted measurements. You need to be aware of distorted measurements, and of the three ways to handle them:

1. Accept the distortion. After all, you know it is limited to the "write job description" task only.

2. Estimate the rate of necessary clarifications and their average time. Enter these estimates by hand into the database. (Of course, now you have adopted the same practice and the same disadvantage as conventional organizational process management.)

3. Represent Christine's inquiries as a human workflow in the process engine. Then you can measure and analyze the respective rates and times in a differentiated manner. The risk is that neither Christine nor Falko will be thrilled by this idea, and they may simply bypass the process engine and settle their questions with a more efficient phone call.

As you can see, process automation is a powerful instrument for process control, but you should be wary of overusing it. We hope you'll also see that BPMN helps us to recognize these limits in time and to prepare for them.

On the other hand, we have to understand that BPMN in its "raw" form does not provide sufficient support for process analysis based on key figures. You can only do this with a powerful BPMN tool that takes in the key figures —ideally from the process engine —and aggregates them for functional analysis. It can do this usefully because you are a master at producing consistent process models.

4.5.1.2   Explicit modeling of errors

Unlike other notations, BPMN explicitly models errors with event types (section 2.6.4 on page 43). It is only a question of when to use them. In the last section, we discussed correction loops that apply only in case of errors. You would not want to use error events in those cases, because you want to reserve error events for representing activities that *cannot* complete successfully. If an activity can complete, but the *result* differs from what was expected, that's different. It isn't always clear what every situation calls for, and there can be gray areas. Let's look at a simple example.

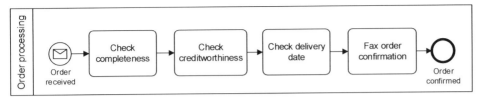

FIGURE 4.19 Happy path order processing.

Figure 4.19 shows the happy path for order processing. There are four steps: For a new order, the order processor checks the order form for completeness, then he or she checks the customer's credit. The date of delivery is checked, and finally, the processor faxes a confirmation.

Now we imagine what can go wrong, what the response is going to be in each case, and how to represent these possibilities in the process model. To think it through, we start at the end and work backwards. The happy path result was that the order was confirmed, so what could lead to the order *not* being confirmed? Yes, theoretically, anything can happen —even an earthquake —but practicality suggests that we deal in events with higher levels of probability. We decide on the following:

1. The order details are incomplete.
2. The order details are illegible.
3. The customer ID is wrong.
4. The customer has insufficient credit.
5. The ordered item is not available.
6. When faxing the order confirmation, someone answers the phone and asks our fax machine if the call is supposed to be a bad joke.

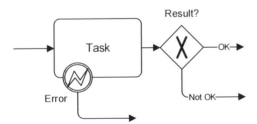

FIGURE 4.20 Representing possible (and probable) problems in the process.

How would we model these contingencies in the process? As shown in abstract in figure 4.20, a task either provides us with a result, that is, information that we can assess as OK or not OK, or there is no result, and the task can't complete at all. If we have the information to assess, we can model an XOR split after the task. If the task can't complete, this is the time for an error event. For each of the possible problems we've defined, we can now construct error-handling solutions. See the fully modeled process in figure 4.21 on the following page.

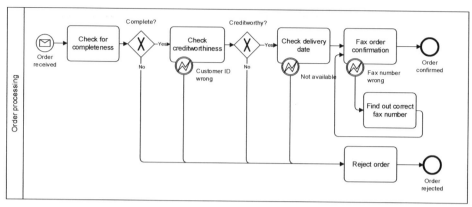

FIGURE 4.21 Representing possible alternatives to the happy path.

- **The order details are incomplete.**

  This is simple: The check for completeness succeeded, but the result is that the order is incomplete, so processing follows the XOR split after the task to "reject order."

- **The order details are illegible.**

  How can you check for completeness when the order is illegible? This isn't as obvious as when the order details are plainly incomplete, but the result is the same. If we cannot read the details, they don't exist for us. The order is still incomplete. (Though may be helpful to explain to the customer *why* his or her order was rejected.)

- **The customer ID is wrong.**

  Unless we can validate that the customer has the correct customer ID, we can't make much more progress on the order. This is a clear case for an attached error event.

- **The customer has insufficient credit.**

  If our process successfully checks credit, but the result is unfavorable, the result prevents the order confirmation. The XOR split after the task sends the order to "reject order."

- **The ordered item is not available.**

  This is not so easy, which is why you need to be pedantic. If the item is not available, no delivery date can be established, so no check of the delivery date can succeed if the item is not available. We have to attach an error event.

- **When faxing the order confirmation, someone answers the phone and asks our fax machine if the call is supposed to be a bad joke.**

  You can probably guess how to represent this.

You may be asking yourself why it's necessary to differentiate between error events and XOR gateways at all. Why not just show all error cases by means of XOR gateways as other process notations do? BPMN cannot keep you from doing that, but we recommend the differentiation because:

- Most people who design processes in the target state consider only some of the possible problems. They model these in "check tasks" and downstream XOR gateways. But when it comes time to implement the process, the IT people come back with questions no one has taken into account, very often concerning situations that keep the check tasks from completing successfully. As part of the required ping-pong between business and IT, we document these questions with attached error events, and then we answer them specifically. Frequently, when obtaining the answer to such a question, new check tasks develop upstream, along with additional XOR gateways. If you placed a "check availability" task before the "check delivery date" task, for example, you could make the error event at "check delivery date" obsolete.

* Can you ensure processes with error events in case *anything* goes wrong? Yes. You can define this kind of extra safety net with an attached error event for a section within a process, or for an entire process.

* In general, XOR gateways differentiate between cases. They can differentiate between error conditions, and they can differentiate also between or among positive outcomes. An example would be the different steps to determine correct size depending on if the customer has ordered trousers versus a hat. So a happy path may not exist without XOR gateways, but positive XOR gateways cannot be differentiated visually or syntactically from the error XOR gateways. Error events are visually less ambiguous. Provided you have the appropriate tooling, you can even use them to switch between a simplified, happy path view and the complete view of the process.

The bottom line: Error events can be a good aid when modeling processes, and you should make use of them.

4.5.2   The true benefit of subprocesses

By now, you know the several levels of our BPMN framework, and how the levels use models with different amounts of detail. At the operational level, we also work with different views of the same process to show only the aspect of the model that is most useful to the people affected.

Have you wondered what role the BPMN symbol for subprocess plays in this framework? We show in section 2.8 on page 59 that subprocesses have three main purposes in BPMN:

* To hide the complexity of detailed sequences. Collapsed subprocesses make diagrams more clear.

* To make sequences modular, and thus reusable.

* To define a scope within a process and then define how the process reacts to catching events for the scope by attaching the events.

You can benefit from all these advantages for both strategic and operational process models. For instance, in the process model for "Job advertisement," we defined the "publish advertisement" subprocess in the technical flow, that is, in the process engine's pool. This avoided overloading the diagram with interface calls (figure 4.13 on page 123). Another option would be to define error processing for the entire subprocess by attaching an error event. Because we likely won't need this subprocess later, we should not define it as global in our BPMN tool. Because the subprocess is embedded, and no longer an independent module, it can be collapsed for clarity.

In BPMN, subprocesses are seldom used to indicate organizational refinements of a process. This is why we often mix tasks and subprocesses in the same diagram. Some process modelers who've trained in other methods may see this mix as an improper or unattractive mixing of granular levels. They may prefer to reserve subprocesses for refining content, or they want to organize their process models by making all subprocesses equally complex. As far as BPMN is concerned, we say forget that! These other views of subprocesses make sense, if at all, only at the level of process landscapes, and that is removed from the examination of individual processes. In your process maps, you can make wonderful process groups or clusters. You can even organize them hierarchically —but don't do that when dealing with an individual end-to-end process.

To be effective with BPMN, it is important to understand that subprocesses are a purely technical construct. They cannot be assigned any content-related degree of complexity. You can define a "sales" subprocess as easily as one called "tie shoelaces." Collapse both subprocess within the same diagram —it's all good.

While it is highly probable that more subprocesses are defined at the strategic level than at the operational level in our framework, this isn't obligatory. You can apply both these levels of our framework to finely granular processes of any type. The framework merely facilitates transition from a general, result-oriented process representation (organizational implementation) to the actual technical implementation. Just like tasks, subprocesses can help at every level.

4.5.3   The limits of formalization

BPMN is based on the assumption that we can define a process sequence as an unambiguous control flow. As we add detail to a target state process in BPMN, we limit the range of people's actions within the process. A total application of this paradigm would equate to an industrial assembly line that leaves its participants with no creative freedom at all. There are Internet forums dedicated to opposing BPM on humanitarian grounds, to resisting what they see as increasingly technocratic control on society. This issue is out-of-scope for this book, but we offer a pragmatic observation: We often have had to accept "white spots" in process models, things that simply could not be made clear as part of an actual state survey or a target state design. There seems to be one negative and one positive cause for white spots:

* In the negative case, the knowledge of exactly how the subprocess is or should be handled does not exist or is not available. All we know is that we want to change it.

* In the positive case, the subprocess is handled perfectly by the people doing the job, using the implicit knowledge in their minds. We accept that.

In the first case, we have to document an undesired intermediate result when modeling the process. In the second case, we document a desired final condition. What will help in both cases is the ad hoc subprocess, which we described in section 2.8.4 on page 66. Consider the example in figure 4.22 on the facing page.

Ad hoc subprocesses are a kind of "carte blanche" for the process analyst. They indicate which tasks can execute once the subprocesses have completed, but they do it in a non-binding way. How many times ad hoc subprocesses happen, the order in which they happen, or even if they execute at all is left to the discretion of the participant. You can also use the ad hoc subprocess to isolate unclear sections of an actual-state survey or a

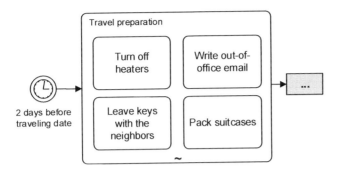

FIGURE 4.22 Travel preparation can, but does not need to, include these tasks.

target-state design from the surrounding processes. We are grateful for the ad hoc subprocess, and we use it often in our BPM projects.

If you want to automate an ad hoc subprocess, that can be difficult. This is also where we quickly get mixed up with disciplines such as case management, which can't always be represented in a process engine. In a way, an ad hoc subprocess *can* correspond to a typical UML use case diagram, one that simply lists the functions a user can call from his or her software without specifying any order. It is also possible to create a white spot with an ad hoc subprocess to represent something in the automated process that can be neither monitored nor controlled by the process engine.

Regarding case management: In the summer of 2014, the OMG passed the standard CMMN (Case Management Model and Notation). This standard is similar to BPMN, but instead of structured processes, it focuses on "cases," where the precise handling is difficult to predict. In our Open Source BPM platform, "camunda BPM," we implement the new standard to provide the option of combining BPMN processes with CMMN cases. To stay current on development, see the project web site: http://camunda.org.

4.5.4 Retrieve business rules from processes

We examined the "order processing" process in section 4.5.1.2 on page 130, and we discussed the errors that can occur while the process executes. Now we want to know which conditions actually require us to check the customer's credit. Perhaps this issue only applies if the order exceeds a certain amount. If so, we define the first step as "Check order details" (see figure 4.23).

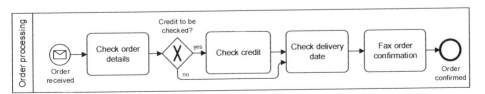

FIGURE 4.23 Order processing including credit check under certain conditions.

Let's say the following conditions apply:

* Credit needs to be checked for any order, the value of which exceeds EUR 300,000.
* For new customers, we must check credit for any order greater than EUR 50,000.
* If the customer qualifies as class A, we don't need to check credit at all.

We model these conditions in figure 4.24.

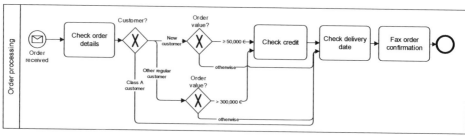

FIGURE 4.24 Conditions leading to the credit check.

Supposing that more conditions may be added, you may see problems with this:

* Each new condition inflates the diagram by another gateway and more branches.
* The inflation gets worse when conditions interlace (in our example, the customer type and the order value).
* The process diagram quickly becomes confusing.
* If conditions change, or if new conditions are added or old ones cease to apply, the diagram must be changed. That's a problem when there are so many symbols and branches to rearrange.
* If the customer's credit is to be checked by other processes, you'll have to model and maintain these conditions redundantly.

Basically, this handling of complex decisive conditions is far from best practice. It is, however, a mistake typical of process modeling. To avoid it, you have to understand conditions as "business rules" distinct from routing rules.

Business rules express the conditions under which participants do or don't do certain tasks. The central, simple, and flexible management of these rules is a decisive factor in the success of process management. Business Rules Management is a discipline of its own. There is even Business Rules Group with a manifesto calling for strict separation of business rules from processes.

To separate business and routing rules in a model, first choose a suitable medium to model the rules. For simple rules, we usually apply decision charts. They require no special software and are readily understood by anyone. You could even describe the rules in words, though there are some powerful notations and tools in the form of Business Rules Management Systems (BRMS). We examine those briefly examine in section 5.8 on page 176.

We made a decision chart for the customer credit question. See figure 4.25 on the next page.

Conditions		Decision
Customer type	**Order value**	**Check credit?**
Class A customer	unimportant	NO
Other regular customer	> 300,000 €	YES
	≤ 300,000 €	NO
New customer	≥ 50,000 €	YES
	< 50,000 €	NO

FIGURE 4.25 Decision chart for the check credit question.

When you express the conditions, proceed with strict formality:

* Bad: "If the length of the copied order number is greater than 10 digits ..."

* Better: "If number of digits (order number) > 10 ..."

Greater formality reduces the risk of misconception always associated with natural language. It also helps to create rules in a way that can be interpreted by software as well as by people.

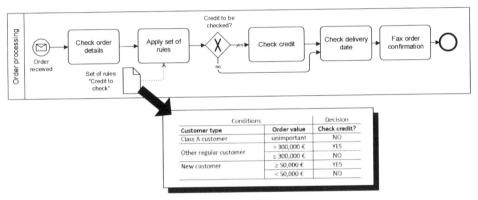

FIGURE 4.26 Order processing, with reference to its decision chart.

How do we merge a decision chart with a process model? See figure 4.26:

* We inserted a task before the XOR gateway solely for applying the defined rules.

* The result of the task is the decision on what to do next.

* The XOR gateway refers only to that decision, and it routes the process flow accordingly.

* We can either link the decision chart directly to the task, or we can define an input data object that refers to the chart.

BPMN-Tooling

Linking the data object to the decision chart is not part of the notation; your BPMN tool must support it. The BPMN specification does allow for adding individual properties to data objects. Many toolmakers use this option, which allows you to store hyperlinks to external files or websites, for instance, with the data objects. The hyperlinks let the user click on the data object, which then opens the decision chart from its centrally stored location. This can work from a company intranet site as well. ∎

Be aware of the differences between the two rule types:

- **Routing rules** are analyzed by XOR gateways, OR gateways, or conditional sequence flows. In principle, they are simple, consisting of the same number of conditions as there are available outgoing branches. Routing rules are stored directly in the process model.

- **Business rules** can be highly complex, and they are always managed outside of the process model. A system of business rules can establish the condition relevant to the routing rule. For example, the system of business rules "credit to be checked" is based on the type of customer and the amount of the customer's purchase. This results in five different combinations, but can have only two possible results: Yes or No. These are the same two possible conditions to which the routing rule in the XOR gateway refers.

BPMN 2.0 defines a separate task type for this. As we mentioned in section 2.7 on page 54, it is the business rule task. (See figure 4.27.) In our sample process, the "apply set of rules" task would be a business rule task, if we modeled it according to BPMN 2.0 and wanted to assign a type.

FIGURE 4.27 Business rule task.

The typing proves that the Object Management Group agrees to the paradigm of process and rule models. With the Semantics of Business Vocabulary and Business Rules (SBVR), the OMG even defines its own language for rule modeling, which isn't elaborated upon in this book. In our experience, we find SBVR much less relevant than BPMN. Also, there is no SBVR-specific extension in BPMN 2.0. Simple decision charts are therefore the right form of representation for most modelers.

Conditional events can be linked to business rules. Unfortunately, the BPMN specification has little to say about conditional events. From a technical perspective, you can interpret it the way that a rule engine checks continuously if the condition stored with the event is occurring. If it occurs, the rule engine reports this to the process engine, which assesses the event as it occurs and starts or continues the process (see figure 4.28 on the next page).

As always, it is important for the alignment of business and IT that you understand the basic principle behind this structure, because it is by no means limited to technical implementation! Even in purely organizational senses, such as legal specifications or safety regulations, the rules must be followed, and someone needs to monitor if conditions exist to which these rules relate. If they exist, then something must be done, in other words, a process must start. On the other hand, it may be that a process can start or continue only after a defined condition applies.

The combination of BRM and BPM currently has the most promising potential for increasing process agility: While the general sequences in the process are comparatively stable, the rules, according to which the process branches out, change often. Business Rules Management now enables a department to define and adjust rules as required. Applying the stored rules by a process engine, linked to a rule engine, causes them to arrive in process reality unmodified and immediately. Business RULES!, as we explain in section 5.8 on page 176.

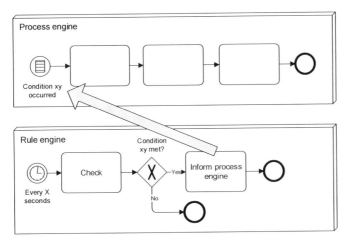

FIGURE 4.28 Conditional event and rule engine.

Business Rules Management has many facets, and there are many variations on business rules. It is worth your time to get to know this discipline better. We can only touch on it in this book, to show that it should be combined with Business Process Management.

Brief side note: That the "check credit" task in our order processing also represents the application of a system of rules should be obvious by now.

5 Technical process flows and process automation

■ 5.1 About this chapter

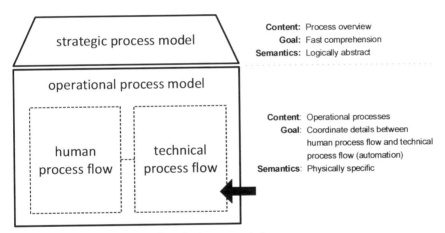

FIGURE 5.1 Technical process flows in the camunda house

5.1.1 Purpose and benefit

This chapter deals with automating processes with software. As we pointed out in the last chapter, you can use conventional software development for this, but it is much more interesting to apply a process engine, especially when you're trying to align business with technology.

There are process models that can be executed directly. In other words, the model serves as the source code for a software solution. If that's your intention, you must remember that the models have to be defined in a very exact and detailed way, because process engines do not understand what "room for interpretation" means!

A major advantage of the model-as-source-code concept is that, at minimum, executable process models always show the actual state of those parts of a process that are automated by a process engine. To change those parts, you have to adapt the model.

This brings up a second important aspect of our framework: if the technical flows and human flows of a process model are linked intelligently with suitable tools, you can keep the documentation of both models up to date! You can display the key performance indicators, as measured by the process engine, in the operational model as process control. Yes, many others have claimed this, but our framework differs from previous approaches in that the operational model must be modeled with precision. That's a major challenge for the process analyst. Many suppliers have tried to hide the complexity in their operational models, but regrettably, that has never worked out. From our experience, we know that operational process models with human and technical flows can facilitate aligning business and technology —providing that an appropriate tool is available. (We talk about tools in section 6.4.2 on page 196.)

5.1.2   Model requirements

Technical process flows must be syntactically and semantically correct, but they also must contain all the technical details necessary for automation with the process engine. The model must be precisely built, it must leave no room for interpretation, and all cases of technical error or exceptions have to be dealt with. After all, this is the source code for a software solution!

5.1.3   Procedure

The procedure for developing the technical model determines its success when implemented. This is where business collides with IT. In our experience, prospects for success depend not only on the process analyst's skill, but also on his or her collaboration and communication with the process engineer.

The procedure typically has the following steps:

1. Clarify the target-state process at the organizational level. These are the human flows we discussed in the last chapter.

2. Decide on the technology, language, and process engine. (See section 5.2 on the facing page and section 5.7 on page 175.)

3. If you apply a BPMN 2.0 engine (see section 5.3 on page 149), all you need to do is refine and detail the definition of the technical flows. If you use another technology, you need to map the technical flows to the language of that technology.

4. Iteratively refine and specify the operational process model if new questions arise.

5. Test and execute the process with established methods of software development.

So far, we've examined only the sequence flow aspect of process control. For technical implementation, it is essential to reconcile other aspects of software technology. (See figure 4.14 on page 124 especially.) In section 5.3 on page 149, we examine some technical aspects still missing in the operational process model, such as:

▪ Specifying data in the desired technology such as XML or Java.

▪ Defining service calls in the desired technology, for example, Web Services.

* Detailing human tasks such as assigning users to groups or determining the forms to be displayed.

Before diving into the details of creating technical process flows, we want to provide some notes on reading this chapter, and also to give a general introduction to automating processes with process engines.

5.1.4   Notes on how to read this chapter

This chapter goes deeper into the technology than any other chapter does. One effect of this is that we present sections of source code that express BPMN 2.0 models as XML. Though we tried to keep the text comprehensible even without the XML, we figured that some readers would find the source code examples interesting and useful. If the XML is too much information for you, you can safely skip over it.

At the time we wrote the original version of this book, there were almost no examples of BPMN 2.0 XML available. This changed when the OMG supplemented the specification with an official sample document. You can access this at http://www.omg.org/cgi-bin/doc?dtc/10-06-02. If you want to study an example that shows modeling integrated across all levels, we contributed to one that includes complete source code.

If the gritty details aren't your concern, you can skim the rest of this chapter for general comprehension, and then pass the book to your IT department.

■ 5.2   The basics

5.2.1   Process automation with process engine

The process engine (sometimes called a business process or workflow engine) is software that carries out business processes. You also may hear this called process execution or process automation. The engine requires a model of the business process that contains all technical details necessary for execution. While the process runs, it creates process instances for individual process cycles; the process engine computes the control flow and always knows what to do next. The token concept introduced in section 2.1.4 on page 18 may be useful to recall here. While not every process engine works with tokens, it is not unusual for them to do so.

The process engine recognizes two types of activities: automated activities and those that require human interaction. The automated activities may be service calls, for example, but they also may analyze gateways and events. Human interactions are applied through user tasks, usually by means of a task list comparable to an email inbox. The list items indicate to the user which tasks have yet to be executed. When the user opens a task from the list, he or she views it through a pre-configured screen mask to view or edit data or to make a decision. Figure 5.2 provides an overview of process engine operations.

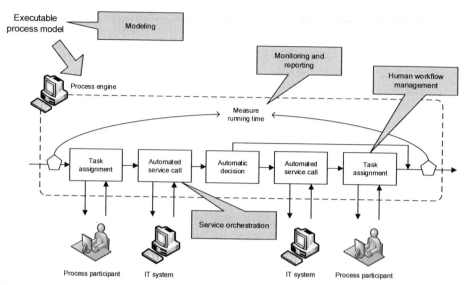

FIGURE 5.2 Process engine principle of operation.

As the user tasks make clear, a process engine has a lot more to do than just to automate a control flow. It has to consider data flow as well. Data can be added to a process instance while the process runs, and the engine manages the data as well as the process state. The data is usually persistent and stored in a database so that it remains available even in case of system failure. A process engine typically provides other services too:

- **Versioning of process models**: Business processes take a long time. An ordering process, for example, may take a couple of days or even several months. This means that when a process needs to change, there are likely to be instances running, and that is why most process engines can process different versions of a process model simultaneously. Transition to a new process version happens by letting the instances of the old version run down.

- **Data collection, performance indicators, and analysis**: The engine can collect data automatically while controlling process instances. We can know exactly when an order was released, for example, when delivery completed, and so on. We can aggregate the data and use it to analyze efficiency or to identify bottlenecks in the process. This also provides a well-aggregated overview of the entire process landscape. Another option is business activity monitoring (BAM), which aims to recognize patterns in real time and issue warnings or intervene with autonomous controls.

- **Monitoring and administration**: Process engines provide options for viewing the status of process instances. This creates intervention opportunities such as aborting or restarting faulty instances.

Process models must be available in a language suitable for the process engine. We discuss the extent to which these executable models can be synchronized with operational BPMN models, or replaced by executable BPMN models, in the next sections.

5.2.2 Execute process models – is that possible?

Once the idea of a process engine has taken root, we often face one problem: the expectation that a magical BPM suite solves all problems. Figure 5.3 illustrates this wishful thinking. If you feed the suite a purely operational model, it integrates IT systems automatically and takes care of human workflow management. At the end, functional performance indicators tumble out through a dashboard, which the business division uses to recognize problems in real time, and then the problems resolve themselves.

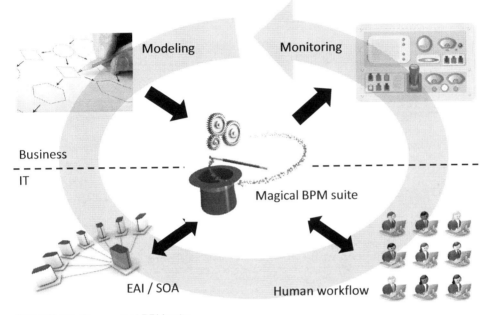

FIGURE 5.3 The magical BPM suite.

This scenario seems too good to be true, and it is. Development of process applications is always a form of software development. The promise that this can be handled entirely by business users sounds tempting, but we have watched it fail repeatedly for years. Even with wizards and forms to help develop model-driven process applications, the wizards and forms are so complex that the average business user becomes overwhelmed.

What happens next? The project lands in IT's lap, where software developers first have to learn how the BPM suite, with all its wizards and forms, works. They can't just apply their programming knowledge because the program language is hidden. The goal of simplifying and speeding up development, ironically, is foiled by the BPM suite itself!

Additionally, two more problems arise from the entirely model-driven ("zero-code") approach:

- **dependence on the manufacturer**: Let's assume that our IT department —with some additional training exclusive to this product —has mastered the BPM suite. Maintaining the know-how implies a constant occupation with the product, and so expertise with other methods and technologies may suffer. If a colleague trained in the BPM suite then leaves the organization, a replacement must be found. The suite manufacturer can provide replacement service, perhaps —for some generous remuneration.

- **restricted possibilities**: Under an approach that uses purely model-driven development, you could restrict implementation only to those problems that the manufacturer's models or configuration options solve well. That may suffice for simple process applications such as the (in)famous vacation request, but it is unlikely to work for your custom, core processes.

Does this mean that using BPMN for process automation is not such a good idea? Of course not. It just means that the right approach —as with so many things in life —isn't as simple as we might wish. In real life, a hybrid approach works. Certain parts of the process application (for example, the process itself) are model-driven while other parts (such as complex user interfaces) are developed by using "classic" programming. You will have to accept that software development in the future will continue to require actual software developers. Seems kind of logical, right?

Following this line of thinking, in the following sections we focus on the technical implementation of process models using BPMN. In section 6.4.3 on page 196, we also describe the camunda BPM platform, which supports the hybrid approach and which is available open source.

5.2.3   Why use a process engine?

Why should we use a BPMN process engine in our projects when we could implement the process diagrams we've created in our preferred programming language? That's a fair question, to which the answer is, "It depends." Before continuing, however, let's look at the issue in a less-than-orthodox way and re-examine the entire topic of "process automation."

As a rule of thumb, you could say that process automation is especially useful for processes with the following characteristics:

- **High repetition rates**: The effort to automate is worthwhile only if an appropriate number of process instances execute. Otherwise, development costs may exceed the costs that automation would avoid.
- **Standardization**: If most process instances follow the same pattern, automation offers an advantage.
- **Information-intensive**: Generally, information-intensive processes are most suitable for process automation. The need to move physical objects frequently —including paper —makes automation more difficult to justify and less exciting.
- **Potentially high level of automation**: Automating tasks can increase process efficiency. Tasks such as the booking in an ERP system are well suited for this because you don't have to enter data manually. Manual tasks such as calling a customer, however, are not as well suited to automation.

Now let's come back to the core question: Why use a process engine, instead of programming the process directly?

- **Transparency**: One huge advantage of applying a (BPMN) process engine is that the process is visible as a graphic diagram, and not only as source code (XML, Java, or something else). This makes the process comparatively easy to understand. It may be, as the saying goes, that the truth is hidden in the source code, but a diagram makes the truth accessible to everyone, and easier for everyone to understand. Diagrams also facilitate discussions about weak points, possible improvements, and changes. Without a process engine, computer scientists seem like archaeologists: they have to dig to uncover how a process is actually implemented. Only process automation provides the transparency necessary to enable reasonable re-engineering. When an automated process runs exactly as described —and this can be evidenced by log files —it is often a great help to compliance requirements.

* **Agility**: BPM and SOA are often compared to Legos, the interlocking plastic toy bricks. As with Legos, you build your process out of available services. As one of our customers observed, however, "Look at today's Lego kits. They contain highly complex and specific bricks, which you would by no means reuse in other places." To build a complex end product like a Lego spaceship, the simple bricks won't do, nor can you put any brick in any position. Does this mean no agility? No, because the increased transparency makes the adjustment of processes feasible in the first place. It doesn't happen at the push of a button, but at least we can assess the effects of process changes and see where we have to intervene. Furthermore, the visibility of the process leads to services of suitable granularity, and so it supports reasonable modularization of IT systems.

* **Quality**: Imagine any mail-order company. When you inquire about an order, there are two possible answers: delayed ("We have to find out first, please wait a moment") or immediate ("Your order is waiting for xy.") A company that can answer you immediately probably uses a process engine that enables an exact view into the process definitions and process instances. Escalation situations due to long waits are thus not triggered by exasperated customers, but by the process engine itself, and perhaps before the customer relationship is damaged.

Theoretically, you could achieve these benefits by building your own process engine. Would you also build your own database? Probably not. More likely, you would use proven products, especially if they were available free of charge.

All right, so you are convinced to apply a process engine. The next consideration is to determine which aspects are expressed by executable process models and which aspects may be addressed better by classical software development. You can't make that determination without knowing the specifics, but there are several factors to think through:

* **Technology and architecture**: Depending on the process engine used and the overall architecture, it can be easy or difficult to implement certain requirements within the process. Some process engines, for example, can implement simple scripts directly.

* **Available infrastructure**: Few projects are developed with a greenfield approach. Of course you should reuse or integrate available systems and services. Then, for instance, you can trigger processes with an existing scheduler infrastructure and not with the process engine. Marginal conditions must be taken into account.

* **Roles in the project**: It is important not to underestimate existing roles and know-how. Projects often involve developers who are able to implement certain functionality quickly with classical programming, but they need a long time to do it with a process

engine. On the other hand, there may be qualified process engineers who can master process models better than they can programming languages.

If you fail to take these factors into account, it can lead to less-than-optimal solutions. It can even lead to solutions that make no technical sense for the target architecture.

In our practice, we often find that the impulse, once the process engine has been procured, is to use it for everything. Overly detailed process models often emerge, in which you can't see the forest for the trees. Such models neither help in communicating with the business, nor are they easier to maintain than conventional program code. IT will also hate the models, and that doesn't help anybody. The point is to strive for just the right granularity. Modeled processes are just one piece of the puzzle.

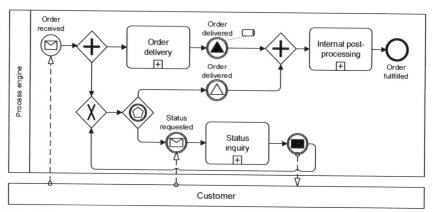

FIGURE 5.4 Bad example: modeling too many aspects in the process.

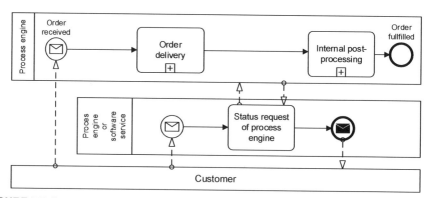

FIGURE 5.5 Better example: the status inquiry separated from the process.

Figure 5.4 shows an unfortunate example. It models explicitly how to answer a customer's inquiry for his current process state. It's irrelevant if we model this process with a signal event (as shown), or a conditional event, or a terminate end event. The process becomes too complicated in any case. Also, it may be a bad idea to integrate the customer inquiry directly into the order process. Wouldn't it be better to model the inquiry as a separate process, or to use a simple service to get the status from the process engine? The requirement we place on the process engine is then: the status of a running process instance must be easy to discover. See the improvement in figure 5.5 on the preceding page. Whether the inquiry is realized in a separate process or as a simple software service depends on the architecture.

Hint: Business-IT-Alignment

The alignment of business and technology does not mean that software can no longer be developed conventionally. It means integrating the process engine and graphical views of processes as additional tools within your architecture. Beware of finely granular process models. Be guided by the operational diagrams, and you'll be pleased to find that your executable models may be readily understood by the business users —at least those business users who grasp the need to create technically executable models.

■ 5.3   Process automation with BPMN 2.0

One major innovation of BPMN version 2.0 is that it introduced a defined execution semantics as well as an XML serialization format. What does that mean? This is easily explained. Models can be stored as XML files, and the specification says exactly how to do it. There are two defined XML schemas for this:

- **Diagram interchange** contains all relevant information, such as layout information, for transferring the model to another tool.
- **Execution semantics** describe how technical details of the process are stored.

We take a closer look at execution semantics in this section. In section 5.5 on page 174 we explore model exchange. Aside from using XML schema for the storage syntax, the BPMN 2.0 specification also describes the execution semantics and the meta-model. This was missing in previous BPMN versions.

To be precise, any process engine compatible with BPMN 2.0 can execute BPMN models. If you are lucky, you can execute BPMN models without adjusting any proprietary extensions, but we discuss typical problems of this type in section 5.6 on page 174.

Unfortunately, it is impossible to provide a comprehensive introduction to process execution with BPMN 2.0 here; this section merely gives a taste. See more examples at http://camunda.org or in the official sample document for BPMN 2.0 that we mentioned earlier in this chapter.

5.3.1   The executable process model

Starting with the previously defined process model, we use it as input for the technical flow (see figure 4.13 on page 123), but we only consider the process engine's pool. Figure 5.6 on the next page represents this process. Before, we did not show that the job

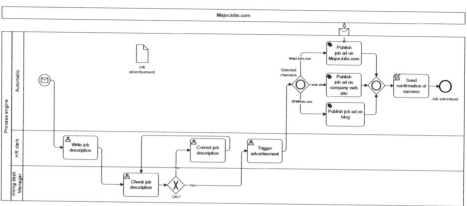

FIGURE 5.6 Executable process model of the job advertisement.

advertisement is executed on different platforms as subprocesses. For simplicity, we embedded it.

For illustration, we also show "MajorJobs.com" as a separate pool, mainly to show the message flow. We will specify the exact content of the message later.

So far, the process doesn't look all that technical, does it? Many of the details necessary for automation are hidden in the underlying model, which is available as an XML file. For now, we want to examine several aspects while introducing the XML format step by step. Because of limited space, we do not cover the whole process, but you can find the full example at http://www.bpm-guide.de/bpm-java/.

From a merely visual point of view, the technical flow in this example corresponds to the technical flow defined in the last chapter. Isn't that brilliant? For those concerned with details, note that we changed two more things:

* We added the "job advertisement" data object because we have to store certain data in running process instances.

* We changed "send confirmation of success" from a send task to a script task. Why? While the confirmation could be sent by different means, it probably will be by email, and the email could come through an automated service or some built-in capability of the process engine. For our example, we assumed the latter, and this leads to the use of a script task in the process.

5.3.2　Data modeling and expressions

In the process diagram, the job advertisement is represented as a data object. There is also the real modeling of the data object in the process, but BPMN refrains from implementing detailed technical data modeling. Instead, it provides expansion points to accommodate diverse technologies. The default setting for this is XML schema, although you could use Java or .NET data types just as well.

What does the data definition look like? For this example, we apply the XML code directly. We use the XML schema as the "type language," then we import a schema file to define a data type ("advertisementDef"). This refers to an XML element of the schema. We can then use this type in the data object as a kind of a process variable:

```
<definitions ...
 typeLanguage="http://www.w3.org/2001/XMLSchema"
 expressionLanguage="http://www.w3.org/1999/XPath"
 xmlns:sample="http://sample.bpmn.camunda.com/">
 ...
 <import namespace="http://sample.bpmn.camunda.com/"
   location="SampleService.xsd"
   importType="http://www.w3.org/2001/XMLSchema" />
 <itemDefinition id="advertisementDef" itemKind="Information"
     structureRef="sample:advertisement" />
 ...
 <process id="JobAdvertisementProcess">
 <dataObject id="advertisementVariable" name="Job advertisement"
     itemSubjectRef="advertisementDef" />
```

Note that not all process variables must be graphically represented in the diagram. They can be invisible.

The specification also recognizes a formal language to represent conditions called expression language. Expressions, well known in the IT world, can extract information from available data. In the simplest cases, they check for true or false. With a data-based exclusive gateway (XOR split), for instance, a token will leave the gateway through an exit at the time of execution. The exact exit depends on the data. Suppose the job advertisement is corrected only if it was marked accordingly:

```
<sequenceFlow id="flow4" sourceRef="CheckJobDescription"
      targetRef="CorrectJobDescription">
 <conditionExpression xsi:type="tFormalExpression">
 getDataObject("advertisementVariable")/needCorrection=true
 </conditionExpression>
</sequenceFlow>
```

By default, BPMN uses XPath as expression language. You can see this in the XML code. XPath is a query language that works directly with XML data. But note that the language can be changed and you could, for example, use Java Expression Language in connection with Java data types. In that case, the process could look like:

```
<definitions ...
 typeLanguage="http://java.sun.com/"
 expressionLanguage="http://java.sun.com/j2ee/1.4/ExpressionLanguage">
 ...
 <import namespace="http://sample.bpmn.camunda.com/"
   location="types.jar"
   importType="http://java.sun.com/" />
 <itemDefinition id="advertisementDef" itemKind="Information"
     structureRef="com.camunda.bpmn.sample.Advertisement" />
 ...
 <process id="Stellenausschreibungsprozess">
 <dataObject id="advertisementVariable" name="Job advertisement"
```

```
        itemSubjectRef="advertisementDef" />
               ...
   <sequenceFlow id="flow4" sourceRef="CheckJobDescription"
         targetRef="CorrectJobDescription">
    <conditionExpression xsi:type="tFormalExpression">
    #{advertisementVariable.needCorrection}
    </conditionExpression>
   </sequenceFlow>
    ...
```

This ability to configure data types means great flexibility when you implement the process engine. This way, manufacturers can develop engines that are lightweight and similar to programming languages —as we have done, for example, with camunda BPM. On the other hand, this means that not every process is executable by every engine. The target engine has to support the chosen technology.

5.3.3   Service calls: synchronous or asynchronous?

Asynchronism is understood to be that the answer to an inquiry can be delayed while the sender does other things. Synchronism means that the sender has to wait for an answer, but the answer arrives immediately or without significant delay. This applies to software function calls as well as to human communication.

In BPMN models, we differentiate between synchronous and asynchronous communication. Consider the difference in the software function call (also known as a service call) in figure 5.7. If the answering message flow arrives at the sending activity, this is synchronous communication. If the answer arrives at a later activity, the communication is asynchronous. You can also use message events to represent asynchronism, but you can't do so for synchronous communication because events always differentiate between catching and throwing. They can't cover both cases.

When implementing a process in software, synchronous communication is simple. The answer is given directly in a technical manner —comparable to programming in which a simple function call returns a value. It's more complicated with asynchronous communication. Because the answer is delayed, it must be assigned to the correct waiting process instance. Now we have to correlate the answer, and the correlation condition has to be defined. In section 5.4.3 on page 164, we discuss correlations in detail.

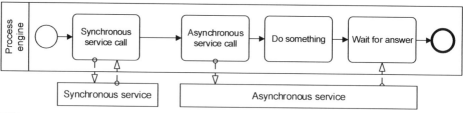

FIGURE 5.7 Synchronous and asynchronous service call.

In our example, we've implemented the call of the online job exchange as a Web Service, and we've modeled it as a service task. The Web Service returns no relevant result, but because it is synchronous, the data enters the job exchange immediately. If an error occurs, the error could be handled in the job advertisement process, and so the process waits for the service task to complete.

We also could incorporate the job exchanges asynchronously. In that case, we forward the message to the system, but the process can continue regardless of whether the message has arrived or if the processing initiated successfully. The IT infrastructure usually guarantees only that the message was successfully sent and that it cannot be lost, so the job could be advertised later. BPMN provides the send task for such cases.

Often, however, there's one problem: communication that looks asynchronous at the business level may be implemented with synchronous services at the technical level. So speaking about synchronous and asynchronous communication can lead to misunderstandings. Figure 5.8 shows a real-world illustration of this. Assume you want pizza. You grab the phone and call your trusted pizzeria. Technically speaking, the call is synchronous: a staff member answers the phone and provides feedback that your order was received. The order processing, however —the actual preparation and delivery —is carried out asynchronously. You receive the result half an hour later.

Suppose you send an email to the pizzeria. Technically, this is asynchronous because you don't know if or when the provider receives the mail, let alone when it reads your order. Things are less certain.

A final alternative would be to walk half a block to the pizzeria, place your order in person, and then wait for the pizza. This corresponds to a synchronous call, because you leave the shop only after receiving the result. While waiting, you can't really do much else, so it equates to a waiting process.

Why are we going on about synchronism and asynchronism? Well, the interesting thing about figure 5.8 is that the synchronous service tasks and the asynchronous send tasks are applied in the technical sense. The technical knowledge of the process may differ in this from the business knowledge, which presumably provided for a send task in both cases because from a business point of view, it is an asynchronous service. The actual

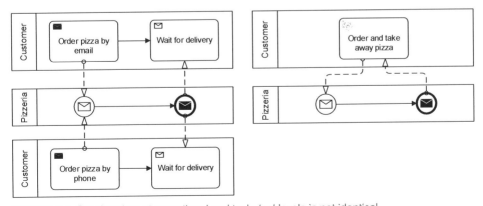

FIGURE 5.8 Synchronism at operational and technical levels is not identical.

implementation thus depends on the process engine to be used. In other words, will it hide a synchronous Web Service call behind a send task if the result is ignored?

 Hint: Business-IT-Alignment

Regrettably, the operational and technical views on synchronism and asynchronism differ. Situations that are functionally asynchronous may need to be represented in the executable process model as synchronous services and vice versa. Remember that.

■

5.3.4   Call IT systems

How can you call an IT system from the process automatically? BPMN's default is Web Services. As we said in section 5.3.3 on page 152, you need to decide from the context if synchronous or asynchronous service calls are involved. In practice, these are mostly technically synchronous calls (like the phone conversation), even though the result (like the pizza) is delivered later.

In recruiting process example, we used a service task to call the job exchange. To call a Web Service, you would define an input message that includes parameters and, if required, an output message containing the result. BPMN provides a message construct appropriate for this purpose.

BPMN is not tightly bound to Web Services, so you can use other technologies such as Java or REST-based services. You achieve this by means of an indirection. The interface is defined with parameters and return values regardless of the technology, applying the previously set technology for the data types. The interface is bound to a specific implementation only in our own mapping. The following shows the source code for defining the messages, the interface, and the application in the service task with Web Services.

```
...
<!-- import wsdl -->
<import
 namespace="http://sample.bpmn.camunda.com/"
 location="SampleService.wsdl"
 importType="http://schemas.xmlsoap.org/wsdl/soap/" />

<!-- Data structure of the message -->
<itemDefinition id="CreateAdvertisementDef" itemKind="Information"
    structureRef="sample:CreateAdvertisement" />
<!-- Nachricht -->
<message name="CreateAdvertisement" id="CreateAdvertisementMessage"
   structureRef="CreateAdvertisementDef" />

<!-- Interface -->
<interface id="Job ExchangeInterface" name="Job Exchange Interface">
<operation name="CreateAdvertisement">
 <inMessageRef>CreateAdvertisementMessage</inMessageRef>
```

```
</operation>
</interface>
...
<process id="JobAdvertisement" name="Job advertisement">
<serviceTask id="CreateAdvertisementOnJobExchange"
    name="Publish job ad on MajorJobs.com"
    implementation="WebService"
    operationRef="CreateAdvertisement">

 <ioSpecification>
 <dataInput id="CreateAdvertisementInput" isCollection="false"
    itemSubjectRef="CreateAdvertisementMessage" />
 <inputSet>
  <dataInputRefs>CreateAdvertisementInput</dataInputRefs>
 </inputSet>
 <outputSet />
 </ioSpecification>

 <dataInputAssociation>
 <assignment>
  <from xsi:type="tFormalExpression">
  getDataObject("advertisementVariable")
  </from>
  <to xsi:type="tFormalExpression">
  getDataInput("CreateAdvertisementInput")/advertisement/
  </to>
 </assignment>
 <sourceRef>advertisementVariable</sourceRef>
 <targetRef>SCreateAdvertisementInput</targetRef>
 </dataInputAssociation>

</serviceTask>
...
```

This binds the service task to the defined interface. It is realized by means of end points, though BPMN leaves these open. The specification defines only the extension points to which you can link the respective implementation. They can be Web Service end points. A connection to Java would be possible as well, as the following example illustrates.

```
...
<import
 namespace="http://sample.bpmn.camunda.com/"
 location="services.jar"
 importType="http://java.sun.com/" />

<!-- Data structure -->
<itemDefinition id="CreateAdvertisementDef" itemKind="Information"
    structureRef="com.camunda.bpmn.sample.Job" />
<message name="CreateAdvertisement" id="CreateAdvertisementMessage"
   structureRef="CreateAdvertisementDef" />

<!-- Interface -->
```

```
<interface id="CreateAdvertisementInterface" name="Job Exchange
    Interface">
<operation name="createAdvertisement">
 <inMessageRef>CreateAdvertisementMessage</inMessageRef>
</operation>
</interface>

...
<process id="JobAdvertisement" name="Job advertisement">
<serviceTask id="CreateAdvertisementOnJobExchange"
    name="Publish job ad on MajorJobs.com"
    implementation="WebService"
    operationRef="createAdvertisement">

 <ioSpecification>
  <dataInput id="CreateAdvertisementInput" isCollection="false"
    itemSubjectRef="CreateAdvertisementMessage" />
  <inputSet>
   <dataInputRefs>CreateAdvertisementInput</dataInputRefs>
  </inputSet>
  <outputSet />
 </ioSpecification>
 <dataInputAssociation>
 <assignment>
  <from xsi:type="tFormalExpression">
   #{advertisementVariable}</from>
  <to xsi:type="tFormalExpression">
   #{CreateAdvertisementInput.advertisement}</to>
 </assignment>
 <sourceRef>advertisementVariable</sourceRef>
 <targetRef>CreateAdvertisementInput</targetRef>
 </dataInputAssociation>
</serviceTask>
 ...
```

In section 6.4.3 on page 196, we discuss our camunda BPM platform, which we have used in many projects. This takes another direction with service calls: it provides extensions to link a service task with Java code or corresponding expressions. This is illustrated in the next code sample. While this is a deliberate deviation from the standard, it's not a violation because extensions are permitted. It is therefore a lot easier for Java developers to handle the process definition. We have had good experience with this approach in real-life projects. Section 6.4.3 on page 196 discusses cooperation with developers.

```
...
<process id="JobAdvertisement" name="Job advertisement">
 <serviceTask id="CreateAdvertisementOnJobExchange"
    name="Publish job ad on MajorJobs.com"
    camunda:class="com.camunda.bpmn.CreateAdvertisementDelegate" />
 ...
```

5.3.5   Start events and receive tasks

Not only can a process call a system, but you may also want to communicate with a process from the outside. In our example, this is true when a new process instance starts. BPMN's default assumption is for Web Service technology. You can therefore provide a Web Service to start a new process instance. This is like calling a service, except that the only data output from the event is the message; it requires no data input. The start event looks like this:

```
<startEvent id="Start">
 <dataOutput id="StartProcessOutput"
     itemSubjectRef="StartProcessItem" />
 <dataOutputAssociation>
 <assignment>
  <from xsi:type="tFormalExpression">
  getDataOutput("StartProcessOutput")/advertisement
  </from>
  <to xsi:type="tFormalExpression">
  getDataObject("advertisementVariable")
  </to>
 </assignment>
 <sourceRef>StartProcessOutput</sourceRef>
 <targetRef>advertisementVariable</targetRef>
 </dataOutputAssociation>
 <messageEventDefinition messageRef="StartProcessMessage">
 <operationRef>startAdvertisementProcess</operationRef>
 </messageEventDefinition>
</startEvent>
```

As with the service tasks, you have to define data structures and messages.

5.3.6   User tasks

The last problem in the example is the human interaction. The user task of the process leads to an entry in a task-management system. To the user, it appears as an item in a task list. The process only continues once the user completes the task.

In the area of BPMN engines, you find three options for handling tasks. The process engine calls some Web Service, which, for example, uses either the process engine's proprietary task management or some internal implementation. The engine can also apply another technology, perhaps incorporating Java-based task management. That's a straightforward approach that often makes sense if the process engine provides its own task management. These proprietary choices may limit the interchangeability of different engines, however.

The third option is standard: WS HumanTask. This is a comprehensive specification that allows you to define user tasks in great detail. It is powerful enough to let you control responsibilities, delegation, escalation, and even the meta information to be displayed. You can define a subject, for instance, for a task. WS HumanTask is new, it is complex, and support by manufacturers is growing slowly.

Here we want to show an example of the simplest case, when the process engine provides its own task-management and does all the work under the hood. A human task could be as follows:

```
...
<resource id="ClerkResource" name="HR Clerk"/>
...
<process id="JobAdvertisement" name="Job advertisement">
<userTask id="writeJobDescription" name="WriteJobDescription">
 <potentialOwner resourceRef="ClerkResource"/>
</userTask>
...
```

■ 5.4   One more word on execution semantics

After skimming the first example, we want to take a closer look at some of its aspects. This book cannot provide an understanding of the execution semantics complete in all details. What we have done is to pick the issues we think are the most interesting, and to discuss the core elements of BPMN within the scope of automation.

5.4.1   Start events and process instantiation

We already know that start events start new process instances, but how do they do it? If you are an IT person, you may think of the following possibilities:

- The instantiation is modeled in the process or as a separate process; either way, the process engine starts it.
- Another IT component starts the instantiation externally.

Imagine that a new process instance is initiated as soon as an email is received. Somehow this email must be technically retrieved, the data read from it, and the respective process instance started. You can model these things as a process as shown in figure 5.9. The process engine would retrieve and process new emails every minute.

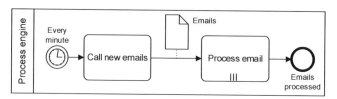

FIGURE 5.9 Modeling process instantiation in the process by means of regular email retrieval.

Alternatively, if IT components capable of retrieving and processing emails are already available in the organization, those components can receive new email and start a process instance that will work with the email directly. We show this in figure 5.10. If no email arrives, the process never instantiates. In practice, an upstream Enterprise Service Bus (ESB) or a similar component often assumes this task.

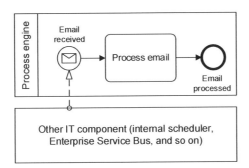

FIGURE 5.10 Process instantiation takes place outside of the process engine.

Both instantiation paradigms occur in our projects. Depending on the process engine, project size, project environment, and technology, one variant of both or maybe even a mixture of both variants is chosen. In larger projects, in which the process engine is a component of the IT architecture, maybe within the scope of Serviceorientied Architecture (SOA), the external way often is taken; in smaller projects, which are very process-engine-driven, the engine handles all the tasks.

Both alternatives have pros and cons. Modeling in the process is often easier, and it may mean that more aspects of the process can be handled from a central place. On the other hand, external instantiation is more flexible and places less demand on the process engine. External instantiation also frees the process from technical details such as whether the trigger is an email, JMS, or X.400 message. Make such decisions in the context of each situation. Do it deliberately, and with the required target architecture in mind.

One final note: the timer event is a special case because it is an "active" event. (The pure message event, as a counter-example, cannot itself become active.) Nevertheless, the event can be modeled in the process. The arrival of a message may signify that a Web Service call is accepted. This is supported explicitly by BPMN as shown in section 5.3.5 on page 157.

5.4.1.1   Multiple start events

Section 2.6 on page 36 suggested situations in which multiple start events must be provided to start a process. This problem is worse in process automation than in operational modeling, because the semantics need to be defined precisely for technological implementation.

Figure 5.11 on the following page contains an example. A broker accepts sell orders and buy orders. Assume that buyer and seller do not know each other and also that the product (shares, for example) need not be auctioned before they can be sold. If a buy order arrives first, the upper token runs to the AND merge. A process instance can complete successfully only if a sell order is also available. The trick of the parallel event-based gateway is that it can correlate the following events: if an offer is received, there's a check to see if the offer matches the existing process instance containing our order. A new token then goes to the existing process instance, and our process in the AND merge can continue. If the offer was not a match, a new process instance starts, and it then waits for the order.

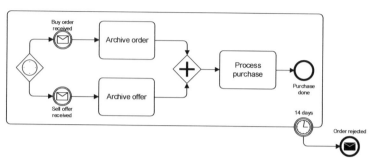

FIGURE 5.11 Example of a parallel, event-based gateway for process instantiation.

From the perspective of the process engine, a major problem is that the process instance may "starve" if a second message never arrives. You should take this kind of circumstance into account. Our approach was to attach a timer event.

Figure 5.12 shows different possibilities for multiple start events. Our example belongs to group (d). Group (c) should, by the way, represent the same situation regarding content, and we allowed for this in the operational model. This pattern is invalid for automation, however, since the AND merge cannot correlate. Besides, the result was two process instances, neither of which could end even if offer and order matched. You have to model with considerable precision in process automation so as not to confuse the process engine.

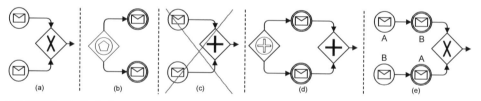

FIGURE 5.12 Start of a process instance by a multiple start event.

Bear in mind that groups (a) and (b) in figure 5.12 show that either one or the other event starts the process. It does not matter if the exclusive event-based gateway is applied or not. So why does this construct exist? Surveys show that some people understand process models better if they have exactly one start node. The gateway serves that purpose.

Regarding group (e), this is another possibility to start a process with two events. You have to model the various combinations in the order of events separately. That way, either offer or order can start the process and the other message can be correlated.

You can find a theoretical discussion of the problems of process instantiation (with BPMN 1.2) in [DM08], which suggests a corresponding external process factory. The process is therefore not instantiated by the process engine itself.

5.4.2   Events and their implementation in IT

Events deserve a closer look from the automation perspective. First, we examine the explosion semantics mentioned in section 2.6 on page 36. Remember that arriving events "explode" if no process instance waits for them. Consider the upper portion of figure 5.13. An order is forwarded for delivery scheduling, but the invoice is sent first. Suppose that although the order itself is ready for immediate delivery, invoicing is a manual task that takes a while. In a case like this, we don't want the delivery event to vanish just because it was ready before anyone wrote out the invoice.

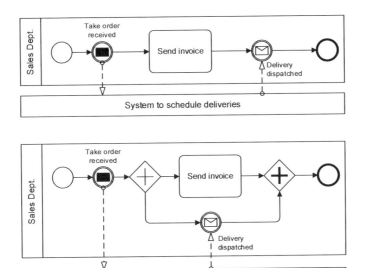

FIGURE 5.13 Avoid exploding message events: functionally clear or use in-house means?

But the BPMN 2.0 execution semantics are strict: events explode if nothing is waiting for them. Process engines have different ways to cope with that, though exactly how it is done depends on the technical implementation. How can you solve this now?

If you intend to implement a process with a process engine, you may have no choice other than to rebuild the model to have a parallel process path to wait for the event. This alternative is not necessarily difficult; we simply parallelize the process sequence as shown in the bottom part of figure 5.13. From the IT perspective, this rearrangement is no problem, but it would mean that the operational diagram has to become more complicated. And even this model need not always be coherent because, depending on transaction management, the answer may arrive before the process moves to the receive event. As always, the devil is in the details.

By the way, if process engines implement a queuing mechanism for messages, which is technically possible, this raises the question of what happens if no process ever retrieves the event from the queue? The sender of the message can no longer be informed, so the process engine will need a sophisticated error-handling mechanism. The mechanism will have to recognize that the process instance, the one to which the orphaned event could be correlated, has ended. If you think that's not easy, you're right. Sometimes this functionality is moved to an Enterprise Service Bus (ESB).

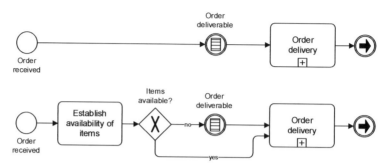

FIGURE 5.14 Conditional event: functionally clear (top) and technically correct (bottom).

What about conditional events? Using figure 5.14 as an example, an order can be delivered only if all the ordered items are available. If one item is missing, the process has to wait until the item is provided —this is what the "item available" condition implies. The operational model is clear, as shown in the top part of the figure. In automation, however, this construct causes problems:

- **Formulation of the condition**: The process engine has to know what the condition is in a formally unambiguous way. BPMN provides XPath as the default setting. But wait, didn't section 2.6.5 on page 44 say that the condition was met regardless of the process? How can this condition be analyzed by an expression *in* the process now? We regard this as a flaw in the specification. There is still a loophole: XPath (or other expression languages) can be extended so that access remains possible from the expression to data and services beyond the process. Thus you can imagine an expression that asks a rules engine if a certain condition is met.

- **Explosion**: The explosion problem might also occur with conditional events. Look at the operational model of the process in figure 5.14. If the items become available when a process instance waits for them, the order is delivered. But what happens if the token enters the conditional event *after* that event already was raised and exploded? Strictly speaking, the token had to wait —possibly forever —because "items available" may never trigger again. From a practical point of view, the conditional event might not be implemented that way, but this is how the specification expects it to be. So it would be better to wait for the conditional event only if items are *not* available. The lower part of the figure shows checking for availability first. While this may be overly detailed from an operational point of view, it might be needed to be able to automate the process.

- **Who checks the condition and when**: The technical question arises —similar to that of the process start —of who performs the checks, and when do they do so? How does the process engine notice the result?

In our discussion of explosions, we said that the conditional event does not check the condition when the token arrives. This is in accordance with the specification. Some process engines may implement it this way, but none that we know of. We see two options for waiting for the event: either check after a timed interval, or obtain notification through an external IT component.

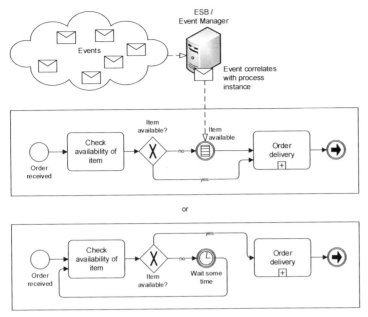

FIGURE 5.15 Implementation alternatives of the conditional check.

Using a timed interval, the process engine independently checks at the expiration of a specified period (see the lower portion of figure 5.15). The process engine could check the expression every 10 seconds, for instance. On the down side, this procedure is inefficient. It produces many unnecessary checks.

With notification, it is an IT component separate from the process that checks and then actively informs the process. This is the first of two possibilities shown in figure 5.15. The checking and notifying could be undertaken by an ESB, for example, in which events like checking for items remains centrally accessible and can be analyzed. The process engine can obtain its information at the same time that the condition is met. This raises the question of how to formulate the expression in this case. The so-called event-driven architecture (EDA) even has internal query languages for events. These problems are not part of the BPMN specification, so approaches to this issue are left to the manufacturers, which means that a process may not execute on different process engines.

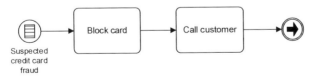

FIGURE 5.16 Conditional event to start the process.

Another complication is the question of how to start a process by means of a condition. In the example shown in figure 5.16, the credit card is blocked as soon as fraud is suspected. But what creates the suspicion? Typically, it is if a particularly large amount of money is withdrawn, or the card is used unusually often, or even if it is used in certain countries. According to the specification, to instantiate a process, the expression must become true within the event. Before another process can start, the condition must become false. The technical solution by the engine remains open.

5.4.3 Correlation

From reading the preceding section, you may have seen that correlating catching events with existing process instances is important. The question now becomes, to what instance or instances must you forward a caught event? There are two general approaches:

- **Technical keys**: An artificial key value is generated for conversations, and the key must be contained in call and response messages. It's then easy for the engine to correlate the messages with the correct process instances based on the key. This approach has the advantage that a key typically is valid for only one message exchange. It is thus unambiguous. That's not always possible in practice, however, because all the participants must support working with these keys.

- **Functional keys**: The alternative to artificial technical keys is correlation by means of context information, for example, an order number. You can also use properties of process variables or messages. You can specify expressions that define how to find these properties in the process variables or incoming messages, with the advantage that no new requirements are placed on messages or external systems. The disadvantage is that the correlation may be ambiguous.

Define the correlation correctly, and the process engine can allocate incoming messages among process instances by means of the correlation conditions. The specification talks about "instance routing" without additional infrastructure.

Unfortunately, correlation isn't easy. Problems remaining to be solved include:

- **What happens if the event cannot be correlated?** As in the case of explosions, when events occur too early, the event usually enters an error queue, and it requires further processing by hand.

- **What happens if the process changed state?** A process instance can leave the expected state —perhaps because an administrator intervened or there was a timeout —and so the event cannot be submitted. Even worse, the process instance is already waiting for the next event and might be incorrectly triggered by it. To prevent these situations, you have to detail the correlation so that it contains the expected process state. That isn't always easy.

- **Wrong correlation conditions**: The worst case involves wrong correlation conditions. These may trigger the wrong process instances. Such errors in modeling are hard to find, but they can be detected by good, up-front testing.

5.4.4 Gateways

We introduced the types of gateways in section 2.3 on page 20. BPMN 2.0 defines an exact execution semantics, which we explain briefly here. "Execution semantics" determines the answers to questions such as: How are which tokens consumed? When are tokens generated in the gateway? Which tokens are generated? Which flow should they follow?

Figure 5.17 shows two simple cases. The **parallel gateway** (split and merge) waits for a token on all incoming flows, and it creates new tokens on all outgoing flows. One incoming token only is consumed in each flow. If several tokens are available in one flow (which usually doesn't make much sense in practice), the excess tokens remain in the flow, waiting for a subsequent activation of the gateway.

FIGURE 5.17 Simple gateways from the perspective of token control: parallel and exclusive (XOR).

In case of the **exclusive gateway** (XOR merge and XOR split), each incoming token is routed through a single outgoing flow. For this purpose, conditions available for the flow —these are provided as expressions —are analyzed in sequence. The token follows the flow with the first matching condition. The order, by the way, is specified by the XML. If no condition is true, only then is the default flow used. If no condition is true and no default flow is configured, this throws a runtime exception because an invalid situation exists. So far, this is simple.

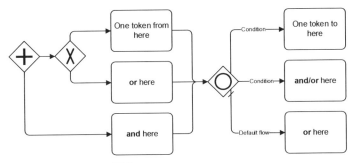

FIGURE 5.18 Inclusive gateway (OR).

The **inclusive gateway** (see figure 5.18) is more complicated. Consider first the behavior with incoming tokens (OR merge). The gateway activates as soon as tokens are applied to all incoming flows or else no token can arrive on that flow. What? No token can arrive? That's a subtlety of the construct that is going to cause problems for process engine suppliers! Figure 5.19 on the next page shows an example of a more complex situation: only after task 2 completes can the OR split know if the lower flow can still arrive or not. We can imagine even more complicated constructs, such as loops, but fortunately this is a problem for the engine suppliers, and not for us users. Nevertheless, use this construct carefully, because it quickly becomes confusing.

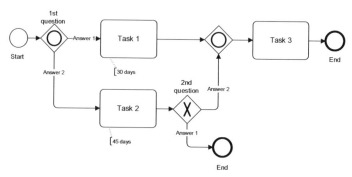

FIGURE 5.19 How long does the second OR gateway have to wait?

The OR split is easier. Each outgoing flow is checked for the set conditions and for expressions as well. If a condition is true, a token is created on this flow. Any number of tokens can be created in case of the OR split. If none of the conditions applies, a token follows the default flow, but if no condition is true and no default flow exists, this throws a runtime exception.

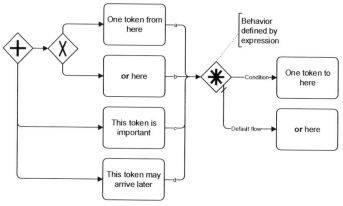

FIGURE 5.20 Complex gateway.

The **complex gateway** can serve multiple requirements, and you can configure it comprehensively. In figure 5.20, a token arrives through flow a or b, and another one through c, which might activate the gateway depending on the conditions configured. If a token arrives through d later, it can be ignored (although that's not completely true because the token from d resets the gateway, which allows it to fire again later). The configuration is put into operation by an expression. While the process engine waits in the complex gateway it even counts incoming tokens. You can use this counter in expressions, which is a major difference from the OR merge. This makes it easy to express: *(1 x a or 1 x b) and 1 x c.*

The splitting behavior of the complex gateway corresponds to that of the OR split, and so we don't detail it further at this point.

But for the end of this section, we want to present an easier gateway: the **event-based gateway**. A token simply stops in the gateway, waiting for one of the events to occur at the outgoing flows. It then leaves the gateway through that flow.

5.4.5   Termination of a process instance

A process instance can terminate under a variety of circumstances. It can terminate normally, or it can be canceled. It can also terminate or escalate with or without an error.

Normally, a process instance is regarded as complete if all tokens have reached an end state. An end state is either a dedicated event or a task without an outgoing sequence flow. This is illustrated in figure 5.21.

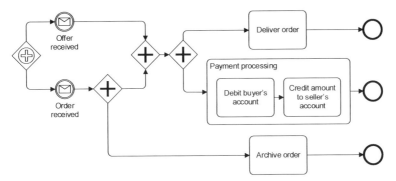

FIGURE 5.21 Normal termination of a process with parallel gateway to start the process.

The process contains several none end events that consume incoming tokens. If the last token arrives at an end state, the entire process instance terminates. This example has one special feature: a parallel gateway starts the process instance, so the process can complete only if all the end events have occurred. In this case, the offer and the order must both have arrived, and even though the order may be archived before delivery takes place or payment completes, the process won't complete until those other tokens arrive at their respective end states.

Another feature is shown in the "process trust payment" subprocess. A task without any outgoing sequence flow also represents an end state, and the process instance can terminate there if no more active tokens are available. A third important feature is that subprocesses always have their own endings. That is, termination of a process instance is always determined at the same hierarchical level, so a subprocess that has not ended prevents its parent process from terminating.

Normal end events end the token, and they may trigger additional actions (see figure 5.22 on the following page). These are:

* Send message (message end event)
* Send signal (signal end event)
* Compensation required (compensation end event)

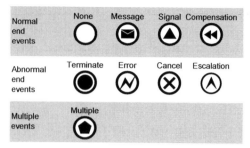

FIGURE 5.22 End events associated with normal and abnormal process terminations.

Normal end events terminate the incoming tokens only. A process instance ends only if no active token exists in any subprocess. This contrasts with so-called abnormal terminations:

* Termination (terminate end event): All the tokens in the current subprocess terminate, and the process instance terminates.
* Error (error end event): All the tokens terminate, and an error is forwarded to the parent process. If no parent process exists or if it does not react to the error, the behavior is not specified.
* Cancel (cancel end event): The behavior compares to the error event, but in addition, the current transaction is rolled back and available compensation tasks execute.
* Escalation (escalation end event): Other tokens in the current subprocess are not affected, but the current token terminates, throwing an escalation event to the parent process. But if the parent process absorbs the escalation with an interrupting intermediate event, the other tokens of the subprocess terminate too.

Only the multiple event remains to be covered. It has consequences that can encompass all the effects above. What's required with a multiple event is to define its behavior for the process engine, as in the XML below:

```
<bpmn:endEvent id="End" name="Multiple end event">
    <bpmn:messageEventDefinition id="Message" messageRef="messageDef" />
    <bpmn:signalEventDefinition id="Signal" signalRef="signalDef" />
```

5.4.6   Business vs. technical transactions

We've already discussed transactions, errors, and compensation from the business perspective. Now we want to examine these things from a technical point of view.

Computer scientists see transactions primarily in ACID terms. (ACID is an acronym for atomicity, consistency, isolation, and durability.) The relevant point is that they want to see a collection of actions carried out either simultaneously or not at all. While those actions take place, the state of the affected data remains isolated from other changes. Writing into a database, for instance, is an atomic action.

Booking a trip is an easily understood example. Booking the flight, the hotel, and charging your credit card take place at the same time, and either everything is booked or nothing is.

Wouldn't that be great? Unfortunately, ACID transactions hardly ever work in the world of business processes, or they work only at a low level. In reality, we have to deal with waiting states, human interactions, and asynchronous service calls. A credit card firm can't wait hours or even minutes to complete a transaction because the required isolation may mean that the customer can't use his or her credit card for other purposes.

When we talk about transactions in BPMN, we mean business transactions. It is important, however, for you to separate these from technical transactions under the ACID paradigm. Figure 5.23 compares the concepts.

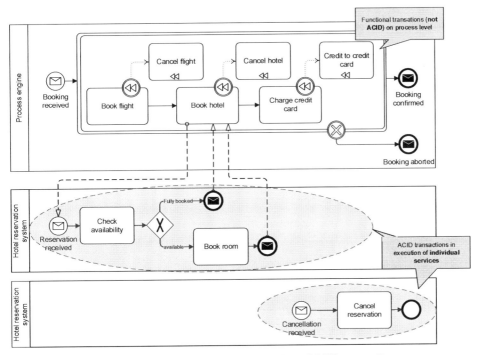

FIGURE 5.23 Comparing business transactions with technical ACID transactions.

The business transaction comprises the entire booking. Technically, ACID transactions normally take place only on the level of the called services —in the hotel reservation system, for instance. Once you make the reservation, it cannot be rolled back technically, but from a business point of view it *can* be rolled back. This is why the compensation can call the cancellation service, which in its turn can be carried out by means of an ACID transaction.

When automating with a process engine, one problem usually arises swiftly: many systems either do not provide compensation services, or a compensation service can itself throw an error. In figure 5.24 on the following page, what happens if the tour is already scheduled or the truck has already left? Some sort of error handling should be represented so that when it's time to automate the BPMN model, the details have been modeled accurately.

By the way, we don't have a good, standard approach to dealing with missing compensation services either. Usually we have to work around the problem, or the

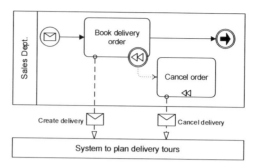

FIGURE 5.24 Compensation in a service call.

software manufacturer has to give in and integrate the additional functionality. We hope that manufacturers will begin to provide more and more compensation services based on the current discussion of BPM and SOA.

If you ask around among scientists for business transactions and compensation problems, you'll shortly hear a term that's also mentioned in the BPMN 2.0 specification: WS-Transaction (see http://en.wikipedia.org/wiki/WS-Transaction). This is a standard that defines two coordination types, and these correspond to our definitions for business and technical transactions:

* WS-AtomicTransaction transfers ACID transactions into the world of Web Services.

* In contrast, WS-BusinessActivity deals with long-term business transactions.

These standards are generally a good idea, but they haven't been well adopted in practice. We know of hardly any projects in which Web Services transactions have been applied successfully. What's often lacking is cooperation between different suppliers —the elementary vision of Web Services. If you are interested in more technical details on transaction management, you can visit our blog, where we discuss this in more detail: http://www.bpm-guide.de/2012/06/19/how-do-you-make-a-cappuccino-in-a-single-transaction/.

5.4.7   Subprocesses

BPMN knows two fundamentally different variants of subprocesses: embedded and reusable. Embedded subprocesses correspond to a scope, and within the scope, properties or data objects are only visible locally. In other words, you can see them only within the scope itself or in embedded subprocesses. Subprocesses are also in scope for error treatment, compensation, or transactions.

An embedded subprocess typically has no large overhead. From the process engine's point of view, you can imagine that the content of the subprocess is simply inserted into the parent process.

In figure 5.25 on the next page, process 1 obviously sees data object A, but not data object B or C. In contrast, process 2 sees A and B, but not C. Process 4 sees A and C only. The error event at process 2 catches errors from processes 2 and 3.

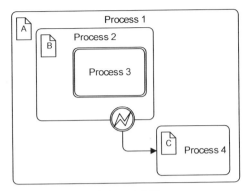

FIGURE 5.25 Subprocesses, scopes, and data visibility.

This looks different with reusable subprocesses. These processes are entirely autonomous and have entirely separate data objects. If you want to use data from the parent process, these data must be transferred explicitly. This is done exactly in the same manner as a service call by means of an "InputOutputSpecification" as contained in the listing in section 5.3.4 on page 154.

Here's some advice that may not be obvious: even though BPMN is a standard, the behavior of process engines varies greatly. For example, when a BPEL engine calls a subordinate process (in other words, a reusable subprocess), this is a normal Web Service call according to the service orchestration —strictly speaking, BPEL recognizes no subprocesses. This can reduce performance because such calls always add overhead, even if they do not leave the process engine space. We have seen customers subdivide their business processes reasonably into subprocesses, but who then shipwrecked during technical implementation for performance reasons.

BPMN 2.0 engines can now do better; they make it possible to call a reusable subprocess without causing more trouble than would its embedded counterpart.

The parent process continues as soon as the subprocess terminates, as we explained in section 5.4.5 on page 167. The same applies to subprocesses. In the parent process, one token is generated for each outgoing sequence flow. In case of an error, the respective error event is called.

5.4.8   Loops and multiple instances

Loops and multiple instances are also interesting subjects. They sound simple from the business perspective, but you can set so many minor parameters that the results are powerful constructs in BPMN. What's more, no one can deny certain similarities to programming languages.

The loop activity is simple. The logic it contains executes repeatedly in succession. The "testBefore" attribute determines if the expression in "loopCondition" is checked before or after the loop cycle. If before, this corresponds to a "while" loop in a conventional programming language; if after, this corresponds to a "repeat until" loop. As soon as the expression —given in the expression language of the process engine —returns false, the loop terminates, and the sequence flow leaves the activity. You can specify a maximum number of loop cycles with "loopMaximum."

The multiple instance construct can execute sequentially, which makes it function much as the loop does, but you have to specify the number of instances in advance, either with an expression or by transferring a "collection" as a data object. One instance is created, and it executes, for each data object in the collection. An even more powerful capability is that it can also execute the logic it contains in parallel (meaning simultaneously).

It is a characteristic of the multiple instance activity that you can specify boundary events to be thrown when one instance ends. Usually, a token simply leaves the multiple instance after all the instances complete. You can instead apply events and specify which event to throw. You can even define complex event semantics to check any expression and to throw one or more events —though this is pretty rare in real-life projects.

What does it mean to throw an event in a multiple instance activity? The answer isn't necessarily intuitive. Consider an interrupting event such as an error. If an intermediate event catches the error in a multiple instance activity, all the instances of the activity cancel. In figure 5.26, for instance, the top-left version shows that an error involving one invoice item results in all items being canceled. That may not be what you want!

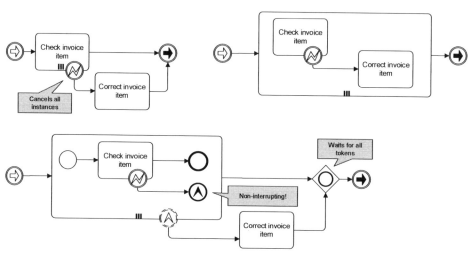

FIGURE 5.26 Multiple instances, termination, and error events.

What you may want is to cancel just the one instance. To make that happen, you may have to execute the error handling in the activity yourself. Suppose, however, that you don't want to process the functional error handling within the activity. Perhaps a participant in another swim lane is responsible for that. There's a trick: catch the error in the activity but pass a non-interrupting escalation event on. This way, the error can be handled at the top level without affecting the other instances.

What about the token flow? Fortunately, BPMN knows the magic OR merge, which waits for any kind of incoming token. In other words, it would have exactly the required effect.

Is it complicated? Yes ... perhaps. But we *want* to handle complicated problems, and if we want to execute the model with a process engine, we must be precise with our models. All the possibilities we've outlined may make sense technically, but you still have to decide what you want.

5.4.9   Auditing and monitoring

Logging the process sequence is called auditing. Detailed data about the execution of a process instance are written to a log for analysis. Auditing and audit logs are an important achievement of process engine automation because in the past, writing such logs had to be programmed explicitly. Normally, engines generically support logging, so the log can be written without knowing the process details. If you want to set additional configurations, BPMN provides an extension point in the form of the "auditing" element. What exactly the engine does with the auditing element isn't specified, hence it is a proprietary extension.

Monitoring covers several things. Technical monitoring of individual process instances is interesting. At what point in the process is the instance? Which data are contained in the process? Why did a certain error occur? There is also Business Activity Monitoring, which enables monitoring of all processes in real time, and it provides proactive warnings when problems are detected. Also, business monitoring is often intended to take key performance indicators into account that cannot be generically provided by the engine. Accordingly, BPMN provides an extension point called the "monitoring" element. As with auditing, there are no details given, so the engines therefore can anchor proprietary extensions as well.

5.4.10   Non-automatable tasks

We have to mention that not all the elements of a BPMN model are taken into account in the implementation. For example, a manual task, one processed entirely without IT support, is an element that is not executable and has no defined execution semantics. According to the specification, the process engine can either "devise" its own behavior —which means to extend the execution semantics —or it can simply ignore those elements.

Non-automatable elements are mainly manual or abstract tasks, physical process objects, and other less-exciting attributes to be looked up in the specification. Figure 5.27 on the next page shows a process with manual tasks that can be ignored by the process engine, though one problem becomes apparent: the decision in the gateway is redundant in automation; it does not change anything in the executed process. Some modeling tool may be able to represent that, though we expect that the gateway will always need to be provided with a default flow to maintain the part of the process that is automatable in this example.

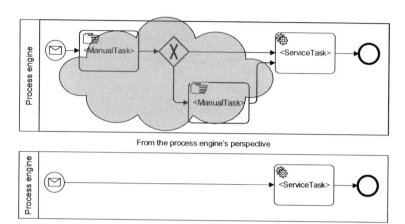

From the process engine's perspective

FIGURE 5.27 Manual tasks are ignored by the process engine.

■ 5.5   Model interchange through XML

In the last chapter, we discussed executable processes serialized by XML. So far, we have only examined the information relevant to automation. The XML contains no details regarding the graphic presentation, such as coordinates, but we want to be able to interchange processes between tools. That is, we want to be able to open a process generated in tool A in tool B. The diagram should look exactly the same, but because the XML stores only aspects of automation, we cannot achieve that yet.

That's what "Diagram Interchange" is for: to serialize graphical diagram properties, and to facilitate interchange of processes between tools without losing the layout. Although information for process execution and graphical layout are stored in the same XML file, the information is separated within the file. It makes it possible to represent the process in different graphical ways.

Formatting normally is transparent to users. It is of concern mainly to tool manufacturers, and we don't want to elaborate on it here. You can find format examples on the Internet or in any tool that supports BPMN 2.0 export.

■ 5.6   Will the interchangeability of process engines become reality?

We've said repeatedly that certain problems may be solved differently in different products. BPMN 2.0 provides great flexibility in terms of the technology we choose, but can a process model execute on different engines?

Actually, we do not believe it is necessary to be interchangeable with any engine. Consider the SQL standard. It has been around for a long time, but exchanging a database is still not an easy undertaking. You often want to use certain features of a certain product even at the expense of interchangeability, and we think that's legitimate. The point is not to overestimate the necessity of changing process engines.

■ 5.7   Automation languages: Differences and recommendations

5.7.1   Business Process Execution Language (BPEL)

Web Services Business Process Execution Language (WS-BPEL) is an XML-based language that combines Web Services to form more powerful services. Services are combined as processes; this is called orchestration. WS-BPEL was introduced in 2002 by major IT companies including IBM and Microsoft.

BPEL was most widely spread around the year 2010. When BPMN 2.0 was passed, BPEL started to obsolesce, although some experts maintain that it provides some functions that are missing in BPMN. Either way, it is obvious that there are barely any projects left that apply BPEL, and only few process engines still support it.

In our opinion, it doesn't make much sense to occupy yourself with BPEL. We do, however, respect the authors of the standard. It was an important milestone on the road to BPMN 2.0.

For those interested in the history, here are the reasons we think BPMN has prevailed over BPEL:

- Control flow as graphic: In contrast to BPEL, BPMN processes are graphically oriented. Functionally modeled processes thus can be executed without any problems. This challenged the manufacturers of process engines, but practical solutions were found, even for complicated gateway constructs. Those solutions may not satisfy theorists in certain esoteric special cases, but for practitioners, it represents a useful compromise.

- No close binding to Web Services and XML: BPMN, in contrast to BPEL, deliberately leaves open the question of applying Web Services and XML in a process engine. These technologies may be the default settings, but as we have demonstrated, it is easy to use other technologies as well. If a project focuses entirely on a Java architecture, for instance, it often makes sense to apply a Java process engine to avoid the lengthy trip through Web Services. So far, this has required proprietary tools, but with BPMN 2.0, such engines can be integrated through the standard as well.

- Graphical notation: Most BPEL tools provide a graphical notation of the process. This is not standardized though, and the block-oriented diagrams are dissimilar to the functional model. BPMN processes have a well-defined appearance that is entirely aligned with the concepts and ideas of the functional models. This is a big step toward aligning business and IT.

We published a summary evaluation on the future of BPEL at http://BPEL.de.

5.7.2 XML Process Definition Language (XPDL) and others

Beside the BPMN and BPEL standards, there is also the XML Process Definition Language (XPDL) of the Workflow Management Coalition. Also, there are many language-proprietary process engines with a wide variety of architectural approaches.

Like BPEL, XPDL is no longer very relevant. There are, of course, manufacturers and related service providers who claim otherwise, for obvious reasons.

We can't provide an overview of products with proprietary languages. We perceive, however, that these increasingly are adapting to BPMN as they issue new releases.

■ 5.8 Business Rules Management Systems

We said in section 4.5.4 on page 135 that business rules should be separated from process models in any case. We also mentioned that Business Rules Management Systems (BRMS) exist. We want to explain how business rules are implemented in IT, which input formats are available, and how business can be involved successfully in this game. We complete the overview with information on how rules interact with processes. This is an important topic in the BPM context, but we can only introduce the topic in this book.

5.8.1 Input formats for rules

Business rules have functional visibility, and in pursuit of alignment between business and technology, the question arises of how we capture and represent rules. Section 4.5.4 on page 135 presents a decision table as a frequent form. In general, we see four important formats:

* **Decision tables**: Figure 5.28 shows an example of rules in a decision table. The columns indicate conditions on the left and results on the right. Each row corresponds to one rule. Decision tables have the great advantage that they are easily understood by businesspeople, and you can use tools like Microsoft Excel to maintain them. The risk is in contradictory or incomplete rules, and while this is not always easy to recognize in a table, there are methods and tools for verification and validation.

Conditions		Decision
Customer type	**Order value**	**Check credit?**
Class A customer	unimportant	NO
Other regular customer	> 300,000 €	YES
	≤ 300,000 €	NO
New customer	≥ 50,000 €	YES
	< 50,000 €	NO

FIGURE 5.28 Rules as a decision chart.

* **Decision trees**: Instead of table form, rules can be presented as trees. See figure 5.29 on the next page. The advantage is the unambiguousness of the tree. No contradictory

rules can be expressed and almost no conditions forgotten, because a dead branch in the tree immediately catches your eye. The downside is that trees with many or with complex rules quickly become confusing, and often, whole branches have to be duplicated.

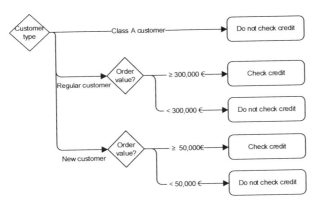

FIGURE 5.29 Rules as a decision tree.

* **Formal language**: Formalized rules, as shown in the left section of figure 5.30, often refer directly to business entities. In the example, these are the customer and the order. You can use properties of these objects directly in conditions. Often, they are represented as dot notations.

* **Natural language**: Okay, to be honest, "natural language" is a bit of an exaggeration. What it means is domain-specific language (DSL) that follows certain principles that were OR principles defined in advance. You receive rules that almost correspond to "normal" English.

```
IF
   customer: customer.type = new
AND
   order.value >= 50,000 €
THEN
   customer.doCreditworthinessCheck
```

```
IF
   customer is a new customer
AND
   order value exceeds 50,000 €
THEN
   check of creditworthiness required
```

FIGURE 5.30 Rules as formal (left side) or domain-specific language (right side).

It is typical, by the way, strictly to separate conditions (IFs) and results (THENs). In formal or natural language rules, the order often is swapped: "Check of credit is not required, IF customer is class A customer."

There are pros and cons to each of the formats for rules. Which formats you apply in your projects has to be decided as cases arise. We often see decision tables in projects; surely this is because of the widespread use of Microsoft Excel. While defining requirements, we often see rules hidden in text as simple prose. Please don't do that! You're not writing a novel, and formal language is considerably more precise. It avoids confusion, and it can be translated into software much better.

Hint: Business-IT-Alignment

Business rules can be represented clearly in decision tables, and even Excel spreadsheets can be directly executed with the proper rules engine. This is a situation where it is easy to achieve alignment between business and IT. Seize such opportunities!

5.8.2   How are the rules implemented in IT?

Once you define a rule, how do you get it implemented in IT systems? We see three possibilities:

* Programming as source code.
* Other special solutions.
* Rules engine.

Most common is to program the rule in conventional programming language. There's nothing wrong with that in theory; software development has worked like that for decades. In practice, however, there are a few disadvantages:

* **Translation**: Rules always have to be translated from the specification into program code by a software developer. This applies to the initial development and to later changes.

* **Release cycles**: Business rules may need to change frequently, but as part of a program, they become subject to the release cycle for the software. With comprehensive testing and approval scenarios, that can take too long. This is part of why calls for agile development keep growing louder.

* **Readability**: The business can't understand rules buried in program code, which complicates functional validation. To discover business rules in legacy systems is extremely difficult. Worse, the logic is usually distributed across the entire system.

* **Traceability**: If a decision is made, it is preferable to store the rationale (why a credit check was required, for example) for legal reasons, for in-house reporting, or to display to the customer. You could, for instance, have the system inform the customer directly why it rejected his or her order. To simulate that in source code is complex.

Do the disadvantages pose an actual problem? That depends on the application. If there are few rules that never change, direct programming may be the right answer. We don't want to delve into special solutions such as implementations in databases or custom frameworks at this point. They are often unique, often extensive, and still subject to the disadvantages we've been describing.

We do want to enlarge upon a rule engine as an alternative. This is in the next section.

5.8.3   The rule engine —what is that and how does it work?

According to Wikipedia (http://de.wikipedia.org/wiki/Business-Rule-Engine):

A business rule engine is a technical software component as part of a business rule management system (BRMS), which enables the efficient execution of business rules. The primary goal of the business rule engine is to separate the business logic from program or process logic, which permits essential changes of the functional business logic without having to change the program code or business process design.

In our workshops, we have been challenged with, "A generic rule engine that can execute any kind of rule? There is no such thing!" Yes, there is. Rule engines have been enjoying a renaissance lately because they are simple and they are available in common technologies. There are already serious open-source products available. The days when rule engines were either purely scientific or too expensive are gone. The integration of modern rule engines is a minor issue, and this helps to explain their rising popularity.

How does a rule engine work? Think of it as a black box, as shown in figure 5.31. An inquiry is sent to the rule engine, and it answers according to the rules it knows. Data is used to analyze the rules; these data are called facts. The facts are usually contained in the inquiry, though they may also come from an external source such as a database.

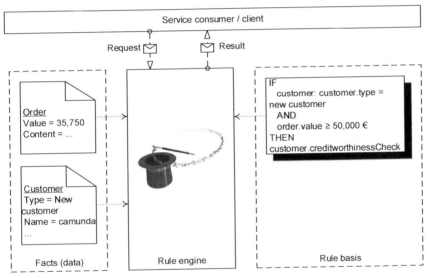

FIGURE 5.31 Overview of the rule engine.

We'll spare you the internal structure and detailed mode of operation of a rule engine, but we can say that there are efficient algorithms available that enable high-performance rule analysis. An example is the RETE algorithm. Some problems now can be solved faster with a rule engine than with conventional programming, so concerns about performance are usually misplaced. Using a rule engine in your project is simple if it supports the technology of choice: Web Services, for example, or XML or Java.

The engine can remember what result originated from which rules. Business rule management systems (BRMS) can manage large volumes of rules. They can version rules (usually revision-secure), find, and often test rules reasonably too.

There is, however, a problem frequently overlooked by business in pursuit of agile rule management: you don't actually want to transfer rules created by the business directly into production, do you? What if there was a mistake, or if contradictory rules were devised? It is the responsibility of BRMS to provide test cases and verification mechanisms, and that is supported more and more by today's tools.

Common tools support some of the input formats mentioned above. Despite frequent reservations, even open-source engines can read-in Excel, for instance, or score with sophisticated web interfaces. There are almost no excuses for *not* using a rule engine.

You can see that we are big fans of rule engines and of business rules management systems. In terms of aligning business with IT, this is low-hanging fruit, something easy to achieve. Certainly, it is easier than BPMN-to-BPEL mapping!

5.8.4   Get along —BPMS and BRMS interacting

Say that we want to apply the process engine in combination with the rule engine. What's the best way to do it? Is the rule engine integrated with the process engine, or are two different engines to be applied? From an architectural perspective, you should separate the two concepts clearly. The rule engine is then selectively employed in the process, and it is called explicitly for that purpose, as illustrated in figure 5.32. A major advantage of this variation is that rules are provided as services, and the services can also be used by components outside of the process. The credit check from our example will certainly be used in other places. In the best case, it doesn't matter from the process perspective if it is a rule engine or conventionally developed software that is hiding behind the scenes. All that matters is that the result is correct.

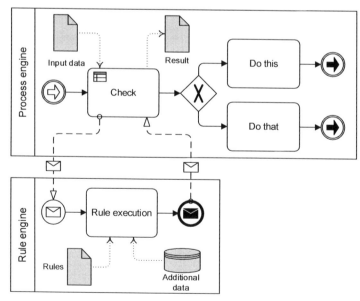

FIGURE 5.32 Interaction of rule engine and process engine.

Our BPMN Etiquette

Business rules should always be written independently of the current process application. You should always try to have another use for them in another process, or even a completely different context, in mind. If you can apply the rule someplace else without having to modify it, you have a better rule, something that can be reused even outside of the current process. ∎

Technical integration, by the way, plays a subordinate role because it depends so much on the technology of the process engine. Many BPMN engines presumably count on Web Services and XML. In this case, the call of the rule engine would be a Web Services call as well, but it is just as likely that integration is carried out directly through proprietary paths of the engine, for example, Java interfaces. That doesn't matter much from a design point of view. But even technologically speaking, separating the engines make a lot of sense since rule execution is stateless, whereas process engines have to maintain a lot of state information. This places different requirements on the products.

Data from the process can be passed as parameters. If required, the rule engine can load additional data independently from a database or other resource. If you want to validate an order, you may need information from the master data for the item, data which is not available in the process and not needed anyway. This separation of concerns is another reason to keep business-rule processing out of the process engine.

BPMN may address business rules directly; it does so by means of the rule task. The technical implementation is given in an attribute with three variants: "Business Rule Web Service," "generic Web Service," or "other technology." Of course, manufacturers will prefer to integrate rule engines from their own portfolios, but we know from experience that it is possible to use and to integrate other engines —such as Webservice —easily.

6 Introducing BPMN on a broad base

6.1 Goals

Over the last several years, we have helped many organizations introduce BPMN, and not just for a few people or for a few processes. Our work was intended to introduce BPMN broadly, and to model processes in a standardized way throughout an entire division or even a whole company.

"At our company, one person draws processes using Visio, another describes them in Word or PowerPoint, and a third uses Excel. Somebody also introduced a BPM tool at some point, but that has its own notation. Now we have an excess of different process models, and that complicates our work considerably!"

We hear this type of statement often as we prepare to introduce BPMN. It is a mistake simply to buy a new BPMN tool and then to expect instant improvement. Even if all a company's modelers start using BPMN as a common language, its complexity can still result in widely divergent models. Even worse, it can result in modelers who become overwhelmed, and then frustrated, and who then give up. It doesn't help that process modeling and modelers are generally underrated. Have you heard anything like the following?

"Most importantly, the tool must be easy to operate. That way, we can find an inexpensive student trainee to interview the staff to find out how they work, and then the trainee simply draws the diagrams. Can't be that hard!"

But it *is* hard. We believe that most of the infamously unhandy process wallpapers from the nineties continue to gather dust in office cabinets because of this misunderstanding. Those who think of process modeling as merely a laborious task produce much paper and little benefit.

In contrast, a successful introduction starts with clarifying and prioritizing concrete goals. This is harder in practice than it may seem because, too often, goals are expressed in a vague manner. A few examples:

* We want to make our processes transparent.
* We want to maximize customer orientation.
* We want to optimize the process efficiency.

All those goals sound plausible, don't they? If you, as a project manager, were given these as directives by management, you wouldn't question them. Our advice though, is to do

FIGURE 6.1 Clarifying goals is critical.

exactly that, and as quickly as possible! Why? Because these goals are not S.M.A.R.T. (S.M.A.R.T. is an acronym for Specific, Measurable, Attainable, Relevant, and Timely. See the Wikipedia entry at http://en.wikipedia.org/wiki/SMART_criteria.)

- **Specific:** Clear, precisely expressed goals leave little room for interpretation. What exactly is meant by "transparent processes," for example? Does it mean that they are all documented? To what level? In what form? For which target group? How does one recognize when an appropriate level of "transparency" has been reached?

- **Measurable:** You have to be able to verify that you've reached a goal. So how will you know if "customer orientation" has improved, much less been "maximized?" Besides, how does that goal connect to your BPM or BPMN project?

- **Acceptable:** The people responsible for executing against the goal must accept it as adequate and attainable. If you expect your team of three people to optimize all processes in a 1,000-person company within six months, don't be surprised if the project fails.

- **Relevant:** Do your goals matter to the people your work will affect? Are they in keeping with your organization's purpose and suitable for the environment in which it operates?

- **Timely:** Without expressing clearly when the goal should be attained, expect resources to be pulled off-task constantly to deal with more urgent, short-term issues. Your project fizzles out.

Almost as important as clearly defined goals is unambiguous priorities. Perhaps your project team can't really achieve all the stated goals. Without clear priorities, however, the team may try to achieve all goals equally —and it may fail to achieve them equally too! Process documentation is a frequent victim of this: Somehow or other, you get it done as quickly as possible. You check it off officially without blowing the budget or the schedule. The result is a sad excuse for documentation, and it ends up gathering dust next to the process wallpaper. It's a waste of time and energy from the outset.

With clearly defined goals and unambiguous priorities, you can discern what roles, methods, tools, and meta processes will be required to apply BPMN successfully. These are the four topics to keep constantly in mind while preparing to introduce BPMN, and while introducing BPMN. We will explain each in detail in the following sections.

In the end, success depends on recognizing what your goals imply. If all the processes within a company, for example, are to be documented to achieve ISO 9001:2000 certification, then the roles, methods, tools, and meta processes you define for that goal will be different from what you define to automate certain core processes with a technical BPM platform. It is also important to take the goals of the BPM or BPMN project seriously, and to carry the project through in all its details.

6.2   Roles

6.2.1   Of gurus, followers, and unbelievers

As with so many things, the successful introduction of BPMN depends on the people involved. It is false to believe that BPMN or process modeling can be learned along the way. They're too complicated for that, and both things require a lot of practice and experience before modeling processes in BPMN becomes second nature. Consequently, an organization must recognize that BPMN cannot be rolled out widely or quickly. First, create kind of an epicenter —a group of top-notch experts in methods —BPMN gurus. These people should possess certain attributes:

* They really understand BPMN completely.
* Even if they don't have years of experience in BPMN, they can build it quickly, practicing its implementation as often as possible.
* They are highly interested in BPMN, certainly, but also in Business Process Management in general, and they support and inspire their fellow workers with their passion and competence.
* They are accepted and appreciated as the authoritative BPMN experts within the organization.

We don't claim that gurus like these are enough to ensure success, but we can say applying BPMN on a broad base *without* these gurus is doomed to fail in most cases.

At the opposite end of the know-how scale are the "unbelievers." Don't worry. It isn't as though you have to convert these people to your way of thinking. The unbelievers are simply all the people in the organization who have no interest in BPMN and who view it, at most, as an instrument for process improvement. They are not keen to deal with the symbols, the syntactical rules, and certainly not the subtleties of token flows. As you've guessed, the unbelievers are the majority of your fellow workers. They are executives like the process owner or process manager, and they are also the process participants who work in the processes.

You shouldn't resent the unbelievers for their attitudes, nor should you think about changing them. Focus instead on how best to involve your colleagues on the front lines in working with BPMN. You can't really expect unbelievers to create meaningful and formally correct BPMN process models; the learning curve is too steep.

If you think of our framework, you can expect unbelievers to model no deeper than the strategic level. Even then, expect that the gurus will have to check the model for quality. It's unreasonable to expect unbelievers to model operational process models, much less technical process flows. *Reading* the models is a different matter: Most unbelievers are able to interpret operational process diagrams after a brief explanation of the symbols (especially if they are shown only their own pools as described in section 4.3 on page 116). So we need not only to distinguish among the levels, but to distinguish also if a given person can create a model him- or herself, or just interpret it (see figure 6.2).

	Gurus		Followers		Unbelievers	
	Model	Read	Model	Read	Model	Read
Strategic model	Yes	Yes	Yes	Yes	Limited	Yes
Operational model Human process flow	Yes	Yes	Limited	Yes	No	Yes
Operational model Technical process flow	Limited	Yes	No	Yes	No	Limited

FIGURE 6.2 Model processes or read models: Who can do what?

In larger organizations, it may not be enough to differentiate between gurus and unbelievers. Just as a religious guru needs followers, a BPMN guru sometimes needs someone else to disseminate the good news, or who can negotiate between the guru and the unbelievers. These BPMN followers, as we call them, find BPMN interesting, but are not as crazy about it as are the gurus. Because they work alongside their unbelieving colleagues, they usually know the daily business well. But they were given the time or had tasks that exposed them to BPMN as supported by the gurus to the extent that they can do process modeling to a certain standard. Followers have become able to transfer the activities of unbeliever colleagues into meaningful process models. They feel comfortable approaching the gurus with questions or problems or to seek advice on how best to model given situations. The followers are, to some extent, the representatives of the respective divisions regarding BPMN issues. As such, they can take some of the workload off gurus and unbelievers alike.

6.2.2   Anchoring in the organization

First of all, organizations should not hire external consultants as BPMN gurus, at least not on a continuing basis. We have been in that situation often, and from a short-term economic point of view, it is not that bad for a management consulting firm. But if a company wants to be successful with BPMN in the long term, the consultant must advise against such a strategy. BPMN gurus within the company are supporters as well as driving forces, and they need to be available every day. It is a decisive role that cannot be filled by external consultants who are in-house sporadically and only for a limited time.

Potential BPMN gurus are likely to pop up in the company's business operations or IT departments. This results in an interesting situation: "Guru status" comes with a certain control over BPM. If both business operations and IT departments exist, who gets control? Things can get political fast, and they can devolve into unproductive feuding.

There's no single right answer for how to deal with this question. Some project organizers claim BPM (under the label of process management) for themselves. No one can deny that IT plays a much bigger role in BPM than it did in the 1990s, but IT experts don't necessarily understand BPM from the organizational point of view. Similarly, geniuses in operations may lack insight into the technical aspects. Project responsibility belongs in the hands of someone who understands and appreciates both points of view. As a general rule, anyone who is inclined to dismiss the competences and concerns of either party is a poor choice to lead the project. The following two quotes vividly illustrate what we mean:

* Business operations: "We have no idea what the IT guys down there actually do, and basically, we don't care. IT has to function; how they do it is not our problem. We only give specifications. It's not for nothing that they say 'IT follows business!'"

* IT: "We sometimes ask ourselves what those ops guys are actually paid for. Sitting in meetings all day long, drawing arrows and rectangles...that's not really work, is it? And then, when they finally give us their requirements, they are so absurd that we can't do anything with them! Anyway, we understand what's needed better than they do."

The only solution in such a situation is to form a joint committee, a BPM Competence Center (BPM CC). The Center involves the BPMN gurus, who act as the contact persons for the BPM representatives from the various divisions (see figure 6.3).

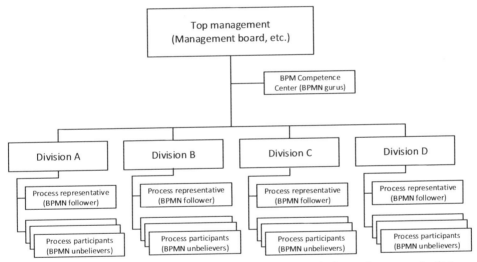

FIGURE 6.3 Typical allocation of BPMN gurus, followers, and unbelievers in an organization.

6.2.3   Training of BPMN gurus

If the success of introducing BPMN depends on the in-house gurus, how can you help your candidates become qualified? Reading this book may not be a bad start, and attending one of our excellent workshops (or one of another provider) also may help. Certainly, humans learn best by doing, so you can't start applying BPMN early enough. Without practical application, gurus-in-training quickly start to lose what they learned in even the best workshops. We have found the following process successful:

1. Read the BPMN book to understand the basics and to be able to assess if BPMN can be helpful to your work.

2. Attend a workshop or hold one in your company.

3. Use BPMN, ideally in your own work, but if that's not practical, try modeling kitchen recipes (seriously!).

4. Optional: Have your modeled processes reviewed and corrected by a BPMN expert, perhaps an external consultant or trainer.

There is another step, not always easy to realize, but it has proved astonishingly fruitful: In initial training, we show typical beginner's mistakes. These nevertheless crop up within a few weeks when we review students' models. For some reason, such mistakes have to occur in your own work before the lesson sinks in. This applies even more to certain best practices that can be applied when modeling processes.

Those most serious about achieving guru status can get official certification from the Object Management Group (OMG). An OMG Certified Expert in BPM (OCEB) is someone who, depending on the stage of certification, has passed the OMG's test. The first test certifies at the fundamental level, that is, in the basic essentials of BPM. About 40% of these questions refer to BPMN and get fairly well to the heart of the matter. You can expect that someone certified at the OCEB Fundamental level to have a good knowledge of BPMN. After Fundamental come Intermediate and Advanced certifications. There are business and technical variants for each level. This depends on where the participant wants to focus his or her competencies. (See figure 6.4.) If you want to know more about OCEB, visit the OMG homepage (www.omg.org/oceb/) or our BPM guide (www.bpm-guide.de/oceb).

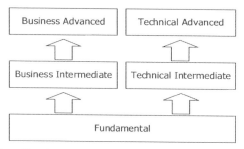

FIGURE 6.4 Stages of certification pursuant to OCEB.

◼ 6.3 Methods

BPMN alone will not be sufficient to model the business reality in most projects.

Documenting the process landscape presumably requires something like a process map, that is, a clear representation of all processes in the company. You then refine the process map until you end up with individual BPMN sequence diagrams. You may wish to link these with organizational charts to show the relationships between operational and organizational structure. Perhaps you'll even decide to write operating procedures down to the most detailed level, and then assign these to tasks in the BPMN diagram.

On the other hand, if you want to model processes in the context of IT projects, you will probably need to define data structures as well as describe the pure process, which can be represented in the IT solution. You therefore resort to UML class diagrams, which you have to link reasonably with your BPMN diagrams. The same applies to screen designs, use case diagrams, and so on (see section 4.4.5 on page 126).

The first questions in the methodical cluster are therefore: In what methodical context is BPMN to be applied and how can the BPMN diagrams be combined sensibly with the other modeling notations?

The next question is about modeling conventions, the guidelines for process modeling with BPMN. It almost always makes sense to define BPMN guidelines, because:

* BPMN is a comprehensive modeling language, and it may overtax beginners.
* You can model the same situation in different ways in BPMN, which complicates both standardized modeling and the mutual understanding we hope for when reading models.
* A guideline is a hands-on aid to orientation, which increases the acceptance of the notation, especially for beginners.
* The bottom line is that guidelines make modeling easier and faster while ensuring high quality in the process models.

Which guidelines make sense depends on what you want to achieve with BPMN. If your goal is process documentation, you will need different guidelines from someone whose goal is requirement engineering for IT projects. Think about the camunda house in this context: The choice of the modeling level and thus the choice of method arise from what you want your modeling to accomplish.

Regardless of the goals, we have established that the following categories make sense in all guidelines.

6.3.1   Range of symbols

For a start, define a subset of available symbols. This helps, especially in the beginning, if everyone isn't familiar with the whole set. For BPMN followers who may not achieve a deep mastery of BPMN, the smaller, clearer palette works.

The range of symbols we use depends on the level at which we are working. In section 3.3 on page 96, we introduced the subset for the strategic level. At the operational level, we normally restrict the palette for human process flows only a little. For technical process flows, the range depends on the BPMN symbols supported by the designated process engine. Regrettably, we cannot assume that every officially BPMN-compatible BPM software product actually recognizes all the symbols.

On the other hand, it can make sense to extend the palette with custom artifacts (section 2.11.2 on page 81). That may seem contradictory at first: restrict the range, then extend it? Custom artifacts frequently solve modeling problems that the default BPMN symbol set cannot solve. We know several insurance companies, for instance, which have to document risks in their processes for legal purposes. These BPMN users include a red warning triangle among their symbols, and they use it whenever it makes sense. The important thing here is to observe the syntactical rules for artifacts and never connect the custom symbols directly to the sequence flow —always link them by associations to flow objects.

6.3.2 Naming conventions

Within the scope of the BPMN etiquette in section 2 on page 15, we enlarged upon the pattern we use to designate certain symbols. For example, we use the pattern [verb] + [object] for tasks, and the pattern [object] + [state] for events. There are situations in which you cannot follow these conventions, of course, though you should try. Beginners especially tend to make mistakes that can be prevented by following naming conventions. Figure 6.5 shows an extreme example. Do you think it's unlikely even for a beginner to make such an obvious mistake? We have experienced it often. If the modeler follows a naming convention when labeling tasks, the chances are good that he or she will see the mistake and self-correct.

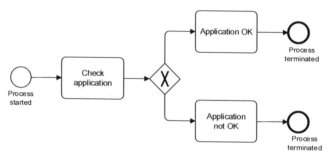

FIGURE 6.5 Wrong: The branching conditions are contained in the tasks.

Another example is shown in figure 6.6.

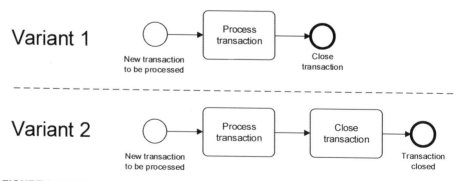

FIGURE 6.6 Variant 1 violates the naming convention for events.

This isn't a mistake, but rather a difference of opinion on whether the "close transaction" activity should be modeled as an event or as a task. You may think that it is clearly a task, but in practice, we find that final activities like this often slip in. This may even be correct for certain end events like the message end event. Particularly in the beginning, however, a mutual understanding on what a none end event symbolizes should be established, and that it means nothing other than setting a status. Without this understanding, some of your co-workers may model the final activity as an end event (as in variant 1), and others may model it explicitly as a task (as in variant 2). In more complex models, this kind of small difference can grow into another hurdle for understanding and acceptance.

When securing naming conventions in a guideline, we use a simple pattern, which we also apply to other guidelines:

- **Specification**: One short, concise sentence specifies the actual guideline.
- **Explanation**: A short explanation helps the modelers to understand the intention and to accept the guideline.
- **Example**: According to experience, most modelers take an immediate look at the sample process model illustrating the implementation of the guideline.
- **Counter-example**: One or more counter-examples also help to drive home what the guideline means.

Other reasonable naming conventions may deal with the labeling of subprocesses, gateways, and pools.

6.3.3 Layout

This category deals with guidelines about the visual appearance of process diagrams. They make diagrams more uniform and somewhat more readable by guiding the sequence flows in ways that do not confuse. For example, a guideline may specify how to represent XOR gateways:

- **Specification**: Always represent the XOR gateway with an X in its middle.
- **Explanation**: The X instantly distinguishes the gateway from other types of gateways, and so it reduces the risk of confusion.
- **Example and counter-example**: See figure 6.7.

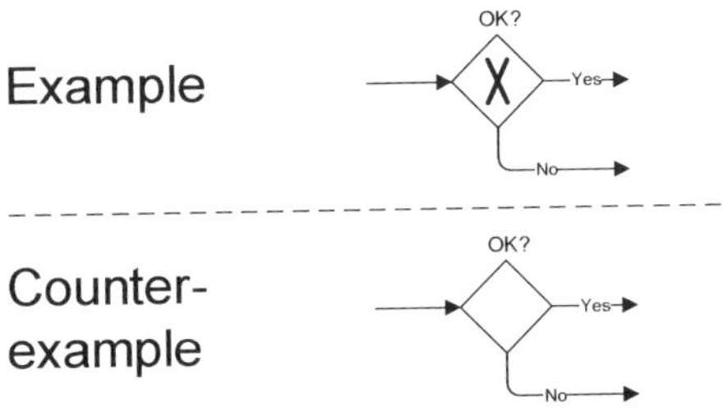

FIGURE 6.7 Example and counter-example for representing an XOR gateway.

6.3.4   Modeling alternatives

While the layout only affects the visual representation, guidelines from this category determine which of the various BPMN options should be used to model certain situations. These situations, however, must be presented as very general and abstract; they should not refer to specific contents of processes or process fragments. That's the case with the design patterns in the next section.

The example refers to applying end events:

- **Specification**: End events with a similar content should be summarized in one symbol. End events differing in content should be modeled separately.
- **Explanation**: This way, the viewer will know faster that different end states are possible, and he or she will recognize the respective state sooner.
- **Example and counter-example**: See figure 6.8.

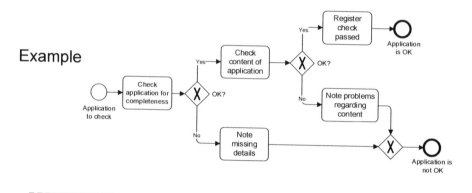

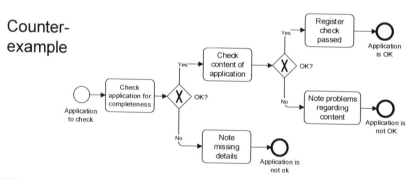

FIGURE 6.8 The positive example has one consolidated end event in case the application is not okay.

6.3.5 Design patterns

We describe design patterns differently than we do guidelines. A design pattern is like a recipe: It can guide you, but it requires some abstraction for the pattern to apply in different situations. Compared to guidelines, design patterns are much more flexible.

- **Requirement**: Describes in what situation the design pattern can be helpful.
- **Recommendation**: Refers to a pattern (from among those that follow), then recommends it. The recommendation may depend on the section of the camunda house that the model falls into.
- **Available design patterns**: The design patterns suitable for the situation are shown through examples.

For example, here are the design patterns for a two-stage escalation:

Requirement

I want my interaction partner to do something, so I send her a message: an invoice to be paid, an item to be delivered, or an instruction to be executed.

My interaction partner does not react. After a while, I remind her of my request, and I may set a new deadline. If necessary, I can repeat this several times, but eventually I have to escalate the process (by forwarding the invoice to a debt collector, by canceling the order for the item, or by informing a superior of non-performance).

Recommendation

From the following design patterns, we recommend "event-based gateway with loop." It is clear, easily understood, and formally correct. Because modeling technical process flows depends on the process engine, however, if the selected engine cannot interpret the event-based gateway, you can instead use "attached timer events."

Available design patterns

Figure 6.9 on the next page illustrates the available design patterns using the example of ordering a pizza:

- **Event-based gateway with loop**: If the pizza has not arrived after an hour, we inquire where it is. Before inquiring, however, we see if we've already inquired. This ensures that the inquiry is made only once. Because the process returns to the event-based gateway after the inquiry, the maximum waiting time is two hours. In addition to the clarity, this pattern allows you to exercise extra patience without having to change the model significantly: Just replace the "inquired before" question with "inquired twice already" or even "inquired ten times already."
- **Chain-link of event-based gateways**: The model behavior is identical to the previous one, otherwise it would not be a valid pattern for this scenario. But now we are chain-linking the event-based gateways. This is less clear and harder to adjust, but you see the number of escalation stages at a glance.
- **Attached timer events**: We can model the required behavior without any event-based gateway by using interrupting and non-interrupting timer events. We would attach these to a "receive" task (see section 2.7 on page 54).

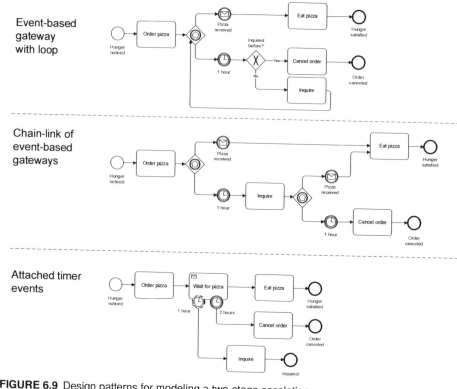

FIGURE 6.9 Design patterns for modeling a two-stage escalation.

■ 6.4 Tools

6.4.1 Definition of your own BPM stack

In the previous chapters, we referred over and over to the typical things required of a BPMN tool, by which we mean a software product used to model processes in BPMN: to show the models to others, to analyze improvements, and to devise new and improved processes. We also mentioned process engines, which execute the BPMN process models technically. A third issue is the development environment that process engineers use to enhance a process model devised with the BPMN modeling tool. This is where the engineers combine the model with other technical components such as an Enterprise Service Bus, entity or data models, or user interfaces so that it can be executed in the process engine. Because the process engine can rarely function independently, it also needs an environment to take care of executing all the peripheral components of the process such as the user interface. An execution environment complements the development environment.

A rough list of the components in an integral BPM stack is therefore:

* The BPMN modeling tool
* The development environment

* The process engine
* The other technical components of a process application
* The execution environment

If you don't plan to implement process applications, and your only interest is in the BPMN modeling tool, skip the next section. Otherwise, what approach do you want to use for implementing the BPM stack? There are two strategies:

* Use a product that integrates the entire stack (a "one-product stack").
* Use a combination of products (a "composite stack", often referred to as "best of breed").

This is not an all-or-nothing supplier decision. There are suppliers who offer a complete composite stack. But will you tolerate the troubles of a loosely coupled stack for the freedom to swap products in and out? The components of a one-product stack may be more smoothly integrated, meaning it is easier to handle. Because so many things are prefabricated, you can develop process applications faster.

With a composite stack, you usually have more design freedom, and you can develop process applications that are better and more highly customized. The components in a composite stack are optimized for their respective purposes (for example, the BPMN modeling tool for process modeling), meaning that they can be superior to the corresponding components in a one-product stack. The single product has to be all-in-one. Okay, maybe it does everything, but it does nothing right!

Are you going to get the source code? That's a big factor in the one-product vs. composite stack decision. Source code usually is not available with one-product solutions, whereas source code often is available for the composite stack. And while cost is a factor, you really shouldn't think about saving money on licenses because of open source. (Just because source code is available doesn't make it open source. Depending on the license, software published with an open-source license can be used for free and even embedded in your own products.) There also are products available for a lump sum or monthly fee that include the source code. The advantages of having the source code are not about costs; rather they are about these potential benefits:

* You have less dependence on the manufacturer (vendor lock-in).
* You limit your risk in case the manufacturer is taken over or becomes insolvent.
* You gain a deeper and more nuanced view into the software. It isn't a black box any more.
* You obtain the greatest flexibility in developing applications for your process.
* You secure the capability to integrate the stack with the company infrastructure: test automation, version management, deployment, and so on.

Using a composite, open-source BPM stack may only interest you if you have software developers who can work with it. This usually means those who can program in Java. If you employ Java developers, then a stack such as the one we describe in section 6.4.3 on the next page, should be of particular interest. Otherwise, you may be better off sticking with a one-product stack or looking to Software as a Service (SaaS). SaaS represents the easiest and most economical way to create process applications. You'll need to accept that SaaS platforms, however, create an even higher dependence on the manufacturer and less flexibility in your application development than do other one-platform stacks.

6.4.2   The BPMN modeling tool

"A fool with a tool is still a fool." This worldly wisdom certainly applies to process modeling, but that doesn't make tool choice secondary or even irrelevant, as some people believe. The best craftsman can't do anything without his tools —except maybe MacGyver.

In general, you should choose a tool that can represent all the BPMN symbols. This way, the choice of which symbols you can do without belongs to you and not to the tool manufacturer (see section 6.3.1 on page 189). If you want to tinker with BPMN before committing the entire company to it, consider a lower-cost solution. You can switch later.

At camunda, we provide two free BPMN modeling tools:

- The camunda Modeler is a simple, open-source BPMN tool available for download. Find it at: http://camunda.org/bpmn/tool/
- bpmn.io is a project we launched in the beginning of 2014 in collaboration with Zalando. It aims to provide a BPMN modeling tool for web browsers. Stay up-to-date on progress at http://bpmn.io.

The tools mentioned are limited to creating BPMN diagrams. They don't provide extensive functions for documenting processes. If you need that, we recommend the following products. In alphabetical order:

- BOC Adonis (http://www.boc-group.com/)
- ibo Prometheus (https://www.ibo.de)
- Signavio Process Editor (http://www.signavio.com/)

All three support the BPMN standard for modeling, and they support documenting processes. They let you export your diagrams in BPMN standard format, which you can then transfer to a BPMN 2.0 process engine. Finally, the tools allow importing, which makes technologically motivated changes accessible to business users.

We have experience with all three tools, and we have used them with our own process engine. We present this in the next section.

6.4.3   camunda BPM: an Open Source BPMN 2.0 platform

After several years of experience in BPM projects and with many BPM software products, we decided in 2011 to develop our own BPM platform for process automation. You can call camunda BPM a technically open source, composite BPM stack intended mainly for developing process applications in Java. That is why we call it a BPM platform and not a BPM suite.

The basic components are:

- **Modeler**: The BPMN tool for modeling and functional coordination of the processes to be implemented. It is available both as a plugin for Eclipse, the Java development environment, and as a standalone version.
- **Engine**: The process engine used to execute the BPMN process models.
- **Tasklist**: A tool to process user tasks.
- **Cockpit**: A tool to monitor and administer running processes.

* **Cycle**: A tool used for the BPMN round-trip, to synchronize the development environment of the IT Department with various business-oriented BPMN modeling tools.

It may seem unusual and maybe even impertinent for us to introduce our own product in a general reference book about BPMN. When we released the first edition of this book, camunda was a consulting enterprise only. Despite the need for really good, all-around technical BPMN platforms, however, we discovered that there weren't any. We decided to develop one ourselves. As declared Open Source followers, we made our product freely available, and we financed the entire project with add-on additional features and support.

The result was so successful that we transformed camunda into a software vendor in short order. That doesn't mean, however, that we've lost our passion for the methodical questions of the BPMN application. Quite the contrary!

Many notable companies and authorities now work with our platform, and they are well satisfied. We are certain that we are contributing to the successful application of the BPMN standard, and so we think it is useful to readers if we reference our product in this book.

You can find more information about the camunda BPM platform in the following places:

* http://camunda.com/bpm has a description applicable to management.
* http://camunda.org describes the Open Source project, and it includes downloadable files and documentation.

6.4.4   It can't always be software

In your first group discussions about a process, it can be constructive to avoid any modeling using software tools. Why?

* Only the person at the computer can model. All suggestions by other participants in the workshop have to be filtered through that person. That's a hurdle.
* The person working at the computer may not have mastery of the tool, especially in the beginning. This can mean delays and distraction from the work on the modeling itself.
* Participants often have too much regard for the process model as shown by the software. Even though they all know it is a work in progress, the inherently tidy appearance inhibits spontaneous ideas, criticism, and suggestions.

The alternative is to draw on an office white board, though this can become inconvenient when remodeling or drawing the BPMN symbols. It gets easier if you prepare movable cards in advance of your workshop. They are easy to make:

1. Print symbols for tasks and subprocesses on A6 (4x5-inch) stock. Use A7 (3x4-inch) stock for all other symbols.

2. Laminate the cards.

3. Attach self-adhesive magnetic tape to the backs.

Originally, we used a print shop for the printing and laminating; attaching the magnetic strip involved some cumbersome handiwork (figure 6.10 on the next page), but it was worthwhile. Participants have used our cards like this:

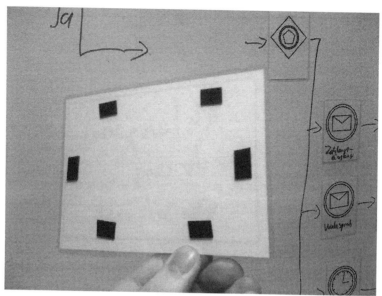

FIGURE 6.10 Card with self-adhesive magnetic tape on the back.

1. Use a marker to label the small cards.
2. Start laying out the process only by placing and moving the cards around.
3. As you reach agreements, draw lines to connect the cards where that is helpful.

Add lines for flows, pools, lanes, and so on only toward the end of the procedure. Doing this while the picture is still evolving is too cumbersome (see figure 6.11 on the facing page).

All this is helpful for exercises, initial surveys, and discussions of simple processes. It also works for roughly representing complex processes or to represent process fragments detail. Everyone can join in, and there is no computer or software to inhibit participation. You can even add custom artifacts. At the end, you transfer this work into the tool.

At the Hasso Plattner Institute in Potsdam, Dr. Alexander Lübbe has developed "tangible bpm (t.bpm)." The approach uses Plexiglas blocks in the shapes of BPMN activities, events, gateways, and data. Participants use the blocks to model processes on a table (see figure 6.12 on the next page), demonstrating their ideas by placing and arranging the blocks on the shared work surface. The result is captured in the process model. Alex's research proves that t.bpm strongly motivates participants to contribute, and the process model they design themselves receives a great deal of critical checking during the workshop. Another result of the teamwork is high acceptance for the solution. For more information, see www.tbpm.info.

FIGURE 6.11 After the lines are drawn, shifting them is a little impractical.

FIGURE 6.12 Tangible BPM in use.

■ 6.5 Meta-processes

In section 1.1.3 on page 2, we introduced the camunda BPM life cycle for business processes and its stages:

- Survey
- Documentation
- Analysis
- Design
- Implementation
- Controlling

These stages can be themselves seen as processes; they form "meta-processes," and we have to clarify exactly how these meta-processes are to be handled, at least if BPMN is to be applied in more than one project or across teams of varying composition. This responsibility lies reasonably with the BPMN gurus. By describing meta-processes, the issues of roles, methods, and tools grow together. We can examine this with the example of a typical process to survey and document business processes (figure 6.13):

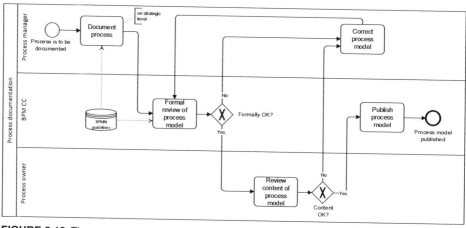

FIGURE 6.13 The meta-process of process documentation as it is lived in many companies.

The background of this meta-process is the documentation of a large number of business processes. The managers of the respective processes, who could be BPMN followers in competence, carry out this documentation in a decentralized manner. They are only supposed to document their processes at the strategic level, because doing so at the operational level across the whole organization is too much effort. When the strategic process diagrams are done, the BPM Competence Center (BPM CC), which includes the BPMN gurus, formally reviews them. Among other things, the BPM CC checks to see if the models comply with defined BPMN guidelines. The process managers correct their models as needed, otherwise, the process owner reviews the content and approves the documentation. The BPM CC then takes care of publishing the approved documentation, on the intranet, for instance.

This is just one example of a meta-process, and it may not apply to every kind of company. A completely different process may be better suited to your case. We only wanted to illustrate "meta-processes" are about and why it is important to clarify them.

■ 6.6 Practical example: Process documentation at Energie Südbayern

6.6.1 Company profile Energie Südbayern

Energie Südbayern (ESB) —an energy provider operating all over Germany —supplies about 160,000 residential and business customers as well as municipalities and local energy providers with electrical power and natural gas. The sustainably oriented range of services focuses on integrated energy and climate concepts from energy production and the operation of energy networks through trading to innovative solutions for energy efficiency and eco-mobility. ESB has a headcount of more than 300 and has been successfully for 50 years.

6.6.2 Starting point and assignment

Due to strong growth, ESB decided to advance the systematic management of its business processes. This task was assigned to the company's division for organizational development, which tackled developing and implementing effective BPM governance. We got the job of coaching these activities with emphasis on process documentation in BPMN.

6.6.3 Project development

In the beginning, we discussed BPM generally, as a road map to introduce the subject and also as a template for management instruction that we devised to get management to commit to the initiative. Energie Südbayern adopted the camunda BPM life cycle as its reference model.

After the core project team completed initial BPMN training, we had to choose a suitable tool. The team compiled a company-specific list of criteria. Because the core project team intended to introduce BPM on a broad basis for the whole company, the process owners of the hiring departments were involved. They helped with the criteria selected, determined which criteria should be emphasized, and assessed prospective tools.

Following the successful selection and procurement of the tool, the core project team received advanced BPMN training. The team also helped define appropriate modeling conventions for the company on the basis of our best practice guidelines. In subsequent training for more than 20 process owners, we explained the relevant subset of BPMN that the conventions defined. This way, we avoided having BPMN hinder the short-term application on a broad basis. At the same time, we laid the groundwork for formally correct models that could be expanded with automation. In addition, we developed and introduced a meta-process for the creation, quality assurance, and release of process documentation.

At the end of this start-up phase, we prepared the core project team members for the OMG Certified Expert in BPM (OCEB) test that would officially certify the BPM competence that they acquired during our six months of coaching.

6.6.4 Conclusion

According to the motto "Helping companies to help themselves," we supported Energie Südbayern as it introduced BPM successfully. Notably, we helped to get the process documentation done with BPMN in a short time. We succeeded at this because we worked continuously to qualify core team members and empower them to handle the introduction themselves. The success of the project is therefore actually not our success, but that of the committed project team. Their commitment means that BPM will be practiced successfully at ESB, and without depending on us.

7 Tips to get started

■ 7.1 Develop your own style

We have explained BPMN and illustrated its hands-on application based on our framework. Now it's your turn. You have to consider what you want to do with BPMN and develop your own procedures and associated conventions. You can resort to our framework, which —deliberately —allows enough room for creativity. So familiarize yourself with BPMN and then decide when you want to apply which symbols and constructs.

It is best to develop your BPMN style not in an abstract way, but rather by working with it, with actual processes from your company. Start with processes that are relatively straightforward, for example:

* Making a vacation request
* Receiving invoices, including verification and release
* Ordering office supplies

Yes, you could start by jumping on your core processes, trying to survey and document them completely. These are wonderfully suitable as long-term undertakings, and maybe you could benefit from them in your next life. For starting out, however, we cannot recommend these as BPMN projects.

For starting out, you should prefer a compact and easily manageable support process, and you should model it strategically, that is, with a focus on operations and results. When ordering office supplies, for instance, an employee urgently needs something. She reports this need, the purchasing department procures the item, and the employee receives it and is happy. Now proceed to the operational level, where you can go into the detailed operational handling, perhaps taking into account that the purchasing department won't order the items immediately. Instead, purchasing may accumulate all office product requests into a larger order. Then, from your operational process model, you can derive a simple technical process flow and even implement it. Voila, you have just automated a process that is transparent, efficient, and agile. You're ready to tackle a more difficult process, like those invoices.

The devil is always in the details, even with relatively simple processes. And you have to be aware that these processes often do not contain all the possible problems you will encounter in your core processes. The bottom line is still what we explained in the introduction: BPM works best step-by-step, and when you have a map and compass.

■ 7.2 Find fellow sufferers

You are not alone. Many people in many organizations already have experience in BPMN. Find and contact them. Exchange information with them.

One way to find and exchange information with other BPMN users is to use the camunda BPM network (network.camunda.org), which may be one of the largest multilingual online communities that deals with BPM. It's free, and you can find lots of know-how among the 10,000 people who occupy themselves with BPM. In the BPMN forum, you can upload your diagrams, discuss them, and ask questions. You can also participate in meetings that take place in your region —and if you can't find one, start your own! Simply send an e-mail to community@camunda.org to get the necessary support.

If you become a member of a network like the ones listed above, do yourself and everyone else a favor:

Be generous!

A community is not just a chance to extract knowledge from others for free. If all you do is ask questions without providing any answers, or criticize without offering ideas for improvement, eventually no one will want to talk to you. Benefit from the ideas and experience of others, of course, but share your ideas and experience as well. To give is not only more blessed than to receive, it also creates more success. Does that sound esoteric? Maybe, but it works!

■ 7.3 Get started

Thank you for reading our book. We hope it will help you to improve the processes in your organization. Ideally, good processes free everyone to focus on the things that truly create value. If our book helps you to do that, then we have achieved our goal.

Do you have feedback about the book? Do you have ideas for improving our BPMN framework? We are eager to hear from you. Please email us at bpmn@camunda.com. And maybe we'll meet up in some of our BPMN classroom trainings (see http://www.camunda.com/bpmn/)!

We've kept you long enough. Go get started!

Bibliography

[DM08] DECKER, Gero ; MENDLING, Jan: Process Instantiation. In: *Data and Knowledge Engineering (DKE). Volume 68* (2008)

[Eur09] EUROPEAN ASSOCIATION OF BPM: *Common Body of Knowledge for BPM.* Schmidt (Götz), Wettenberg, 2009

[Obj11] OBJECT MANAGEMENT GROUP: *Business Process Model and Notation (BPMN) Version 2.0. http://www.omg.org/spec/BPMN/2.0/PDF*, 2011

Made in the USA
San Bernardino, CA
23 February 2016